THE
MEXICAN
HOME KITCHEN

Traditional Home-Style Recipes That Capture
the Flavors and Memories of Mexico

Mely Martínez

ROCK
POINT

Brimming with creative inspiration, how-to projects, and useful information to enrich your everyday life, Quarto Knows is a favorite destination for those pursuing their interests and passions. Visit our site and dig deeper with our books into your area of interest: Quarto Creates, Quarto Cooks, Quarto Homes, Quarto Lives, Quarto Drives, Quarto Explores, Quarto Gifts, or Quarto Kids.

First published in 2020 by Rock Point, an imprint of The Quarto Group, 142 West 36th Street, 4th Floor, New York, NY 10018, USA T (212) 779-4972 F (212) 779-6058 www.QuartoKnows.com

Rock Point titles are also available at discount for retail, wholesale, promotional and bulk purchase. For details, contact the Special Sales Manager by email at specialsales@quarto.com or by mail at The Quarto Group, Attn: Special Sales Manager, 100 Cummings Center Suite, 265D, Beverly, MA 01915, USA.

10 9 8 7 6

ISBN: 978-1-63106-693-1

Library of Congress Cataloging-in-Publication Data

Names: Martinez, Mely, author.
Title: The Mexican home kitchen / Mely Martinez.
Description: New York : Rock Point, [2020] | Includes index. | Summary:
   "Bring the authentic flavors of Mexico into your kitchen with The Mexican Home Kitchen,
featuring 85+ recipes for every meal and occasion"--
   Provided by publisher.
Identifiers: LCCN 2020017031 (print) | LCCN 2020017032 (ebook) | ISBN
   9781631066931 (hardback) | ISBN 9780760367728 (ebook)
Subjects: LCSH: Cooking, Mexican. | LCGFT: Cookbooks.
Classification: LCC TX716.M4 .M3573 2020 (print) | LCC TX716.M4 (ebook) |
   DDC 641.5972--dc23
LC record available at https://lccn.loc.gov/2020017031
LC ebook record available at https://lccn.loc.gov/2020017032

Publisher: Rage Kindelsperger
Creative Director: Laura Drew
Managing Editor: Cara Donaldson
Senior Editor: Erin Canning
Cover and Interior Design: Laura Klynstra
Photography: David Castañeda
Cover Illustration: Mariana and Manuel Arciniega
Author Photos (pages 8 and 192): Leticia Alaníz

Printed in China TT042021

To David A.

CONTENTS

INTRODUCTION

My mom used to say that I was born with one foot already in the street. She was referring to my penchant for getting out of the house to go visit my friends, aunts, and neighbors around town. For some reason, since a very young age, I liked to go out and visit other people's houses, hoping that they would invite me in to eat some of their food. My mother completely disapproved of this, as she was afraid that people would begin to think that we didn't have any food at home!

The reason I loved doing this was because I always wanted to try new flavors. I always wondered why things like *sopa de fideo* would taste different from one house to the other, or why some people would add lime juice to their soup and others wouldn't. So many of these questions about food and how it was prepared often kept my mind busy, and to this day, I still think about food constantly.

I come from a large family, and am the second child in a family of five girls and three boys. As with many families back then, the older siblings were introduced to household chores at a very young age, and that included buying groceries at the market and helping out in the kitchen.

In the summertime, my mom used to send my siblings and me to my grandma's house, which was on a ranch along the Pánuco River in the state of Veracruz. We always saw those trips as fun times; there was so much to do there during the long days of summer. Even though there was no electricity and toys, my siblings and cousins always found ways to have fun. Our afternoon pastimes included playing hide-and-seek and sticking chicken feathers into the top of a dried corncob so we could spin it in the air like a helicopter.

Most of the morning-to-midday hours at the farm were spent cooking. It was a process that involved all the women in the family, each with a specific job in the kitchen. One would be preparing the salsa in the *molcajete*, another would be grinding the masa on the *metate*, and another would be making the tortillas while my grandma was cooking the main dishes. My job was to grind the corn in the manual corn grinder.

Sometimes, my grandma would send one of my cousins and me to deliver lunch to the men in the family, who were working in the fields. The lunch would often consist of a batch of freshly made corn tortillas, each folded and stuffed with scrambled eggs in a spicy salsa. They would be in a pile and tied up in a bundle with a kitchen napkin, almost as if it were a gift. To drink would be coffee with raw milk, carried in an aguardiente glass bottle closed with a small piece of corncob.

Though simple, those egg-in-salsa tacos were absolutely delicious. They were made with eggs that my grandma collected from the hens early in the morning and tomatoes and peppers picked from her garden next to the riverbank. I swear that, somehow, the flavors of those tacos were enhanced during the small trip from my grandma's kitchen to the field where my uncles were working. Even though the summers were hot and humid on the farm, a sip of some hot coffee after those tacos felt perfect.

I never realized that going to the ranch in Veracruz every summer formed a part of my school of life, as it taught me about cooking and being resourceful with what nature has to offer. I also learned what foods were available during the different seasons. As I grew older, I started to experiment with recipes in my mom's kitchen, first with cakes and then with other dishes. As a young woman, I moved to the state of Tabasco, in the south of Mexico, to work as a rural schoolteacher. Because of my experience at my grandma's house, I was able to quickly adapt to rural life in the south. I started to ask the local women in the small village where I lived questions regarding why they cooked the way they did. For example, I wondered why they didn't cook with *nopales* like in the north, despite having access to them, or why they liked to cut the flowers from the trees and make scrambled eggs with them.

From Tabasco, I traveled to nearby states in the Yucatán Peninsula, and with these travels my culinary world continued to expand, with so many new dishes to taste and cook. When I got married, my husband's job allowed me to travel to many other states in the country.

Throughout my moves and travels, my collection of recipes started to grow, and I always kept thinking that one day I would put them all together in a nice, pretty-looking binder. Life kept our little family moving several times throughout Mexico, and later on to the United States. It was here in the US that I finally had the time to start organizing those recipes.

In the early 2000s, I started participating in online cooking forums, which were up-and-coming at the time, and that was when I began sharing my recipes and food photos with others. Eventually, my family and friends told me that I needed to start a cooking blog about Mexican food, because the ones that existed were not representing Mexican food for what it really was. So, in 2008, I started Mexico in My Kitchen. I decided on that name because I didn't want my family to miss our traditional food. If we couldn't go to Mexico to enjoy its food, we would have Mexico in our kitchen!

In the beginning, the blog was a project that I decided to take on for my then-teenage son, so that it could be an easy way for him to find his mom's recipes when he grew up, even if he was far from home. Over time, I started to receive emails from people telling me how much they missed their mom's or grandma's cooking, and how the recipes on the blog reminded them so much of that food. It was then that I realized that I wasn't only writing these recipes for my son, but also for the many immigrant sons and daughters who were missing the home-cooked meals of their childhoods. To them, cooking those meals made them feel closer to home, if only for a moment.

In *The Mexican Home Kitchen*, you will find home-style meals that are cooked in everyday life in Mexico, dishes that people are making today in their kitchens for their families. These range from comforting foods like *caldo de pollo* and *carne con papas*, celebratory recipes like *mole poblano* and *pastel de cumpleaños,* and classics like *tamales* and *pozole*, as well as *aguas frescas* prepared with in-season fruits. These are all meals that bring back memories for many Mexicans, who, like me, miss our culture. When we cook them, it's almost as if we take a little trip back home and sit down with our grandma or mom to enjoy a meal that they prepared with lots of love. You will also find recipes for making basics, like corn and flour tortillas, salsas, rice, and beans.

In Mexico, every recipe can vary from one region to another, since every cook likes to add their own twist, or add ingredients that are local to them. For the recipes in this book, I've tried to give you substitutions when possible, in case you can't find an ingredient. Remember that you're always welcome to give a recipe your own personal touch.

I have developed the majority of these recipes, but a few of them were given to me by friends, family, and fellow food lovers I've met throughout my travels in Mexico. I hope you enjoy them and make them your own. If only one of these recipes becomes a favorite in your family, then writing this book was well worth it.

Happy cooking!

Mely with a *metate* that is used for grinding masa.

THE MEXICAN PANTRY

One of the things that makes Mexican cuisine unique is the wide array of ingredients it uses. Mexico has one of the most diverse ecosystems in the world, and with it comes an endless variety of fruits, vegetables, peppers, herbs, and spices. Below you will find a list of essential ingredients to keep in your pantry or refrigerator. They will all be used for making the recipes in this book, and can also be used to make the dishes you come up with on your own. They represent the most common ingredients found in a Mexican kitchen.

VEGETABLES

AVOCADOS: Avocados are used for making Guacamole (page 129) and for garnishing lots of other dishes, like seafood cocktails, enchiladas, and salsas. In order to make sure you select perfectly ripe avocados, look for those that have a dark green color. The skin should give a little when you gently press it. If an avocado is too firm, it means it's not ripe yet; if it feels mushy, it means the avocado is past its prime. In my kitchen, I usually have two or three avocados at different stages of ripeness and consume them as they become ripe. In case you want to accelerate the ripening process, you can wrap the avocados in paper (brown paper bag, newspaper, etc.) and store them in a dark, dry place for a couple days.

CARROTS: Carrots are used in soups, stews, salads, and other dishes. They can also be found diced in Arroz Rojo (page 132) and Ensalada de Pollo (page 92). In addition to being cooked, carrots are also pickled along with jalapeños, and are sold like this in cans and jars at many grocery stores.

CHAYOTES: Chayotes are commonly used in Caldo de Res (page 28), and can be added to other soups and stews. You can find chayotes in Latin, Asian, and Middle Eastern stores.

CORN (fresh): The fresh corn used in Mexico is not as sweet as the one found in the United States. The recipes in this book are adapted to the corn you can buy in the US.

GARLIC: This is an everyday ingredient that is used in almost any dish. Garlic is used in rice, beans, stews, soups, etc.

LIMES: In Mexico, limes are used in a variety of ways. Their juices are squeezed on top of foods like tacos, soups, and even fresh fruit cocktails. Lime juice can also be used when marinating meat and seafood.

NOPALES: Nopales (cactus paddles) have a neutral flavor and a texture slightly similar to that of okra or green beans. A versatile vegetable, nopales are used in a variety of ways in Mexican cooking. They are used in salads, soups, and stews, and can even be scrambled with eggs for breakfast. Additionally, they are rich in fiber, vitamins, and other important nutrients. To prepare nopales, first trim off the edges using a sharp knife, then scrape all the thorns off the surface of the paddle. Do this by running your knife from the bottom of the paddle to the top (the rounder part) until the surface is completely clean. Rinse the pads, pat them dry, and then cut them into smaller pieces for cooking. You can find nopales at most Latin stores and in some chain supermarkets. If you can't find fresh nopales, you can use the ones sold in a jar.

ONIONS: White onions are the main type of onion used for almost any dish throughout Mexico, with the exception of the Yucatán Peninsula, where red onions are an important part of the local cuisine.

POTATOES: White potatoes are one of the most common varieties of potato in Mexico, and are used in lots of Mexican dishes. You can also use yellow or red potatoes.

SQUASH (and/or zucchini): Mexican squash (light green in color with an elongated shape) is slightly sweeter than the common zucchini you find in the US. Mexican squash can be found in Latin stores and some Asian markets. Nowadays, you can find the two types at Latin stores: the elongated type and the small round ones. If you can't find them, you can always use zucchini as a substitute.

TOMATILLOS: Tomatillos can be used in raw or cooked form to make salsas, and they are also a component in many stews. Larger tomatillos tend to be bitter, so choose smaller ones.

TOMATOES: Most of the recipes in this book use Roma tomatoes, but you can also use beefsteak tomatoes. Both are great for salsas and stews. Allow your tomatoes to completely ripen before using them in your cooking, as they will become juicier and add more color to your dishes. I usually place them in a basket for a few days on my countertop until they ripen, before placing them in the fridge.

PEPPERS

ANCHO PEPPERS (dried): Ancho peppers are wrinkly peppers with a dark burgundy color. When buying dried peppers, make sure they are still pliable; if they are too stiff and crumble easily, this means they are old. While ancho peppers are used in salsas, they are mostly used in stews and soups. The chile mulato is related to the ancho, but this pepper has a darker, more chocolately color. Mulato peppers are used to make mole poblano along with ancho and pasilla peppers.

ÁRBOL PEPPERS (dried): The árbol is a spicy pepper with a long, skinny body, a thin skin, and an orangey-red color. They are used to add heat to stews and salsas. The seeds and veins are usually not removed when cooking with it. When buying árbol peppers, make sure they have stems and are fluffy, not flat.

GUAJILLO PEPPERS (dried): Guajillo peppers have a smooth and shiny skin. They are not hot, but add a lot of flavor to soups and stews.

JALAPEÑO PEPPERS: Jalapeños can be used to make both raw and cooked salsas. They are also used in some *guisados* (stews). Not all jalapeño peppers have the same spiciness, so if you like them to be spicy, look for the ones that have lots of veins on the skin.

PASILLA PEPPERS (dried): Pasilla peppers are long, wrinkled, and have a deep, dark-brown color. They are a mild type of pepper used for stews and salsas.

PIQUÍN PEPPERS: Despite being some of the smallest peppers you will find, piquín peppers hold a lot of heat. In dried form, this pepper is often crushed and sprinkled on fresh fruit, fruit cocktails, and soups. They can also be cooked, toasted, or crushed to make salsas and stews. Fresh ones are often ground in a molcajete (page 15) to make fresh salsas. You can find them in Latin stores and online.

POBLANO PEPPERS: Poblano peppers are used to make the famous Chiles Rellenos (page 55) and are used in some stews and other dishes. They are usually mild in spiciness. For a better flavor, look for the poblanos sold at farmers' markets.

SERRANO PEPPERS: Though not as popular outside of Mexico as jalapeño peppers, you can use serranos in the same way as jalapeños in salsas and stews. Serranos are smaller, but spicier, than jalapeños.

HERBS AND SPICES

BAY LEAVES (dried): Many cooks like to add one or two bay leaves to the water when they cook pork or beef. Bay leaves are also used to prepare stews and when pickling peppers.

BLACK PEPPERCORNS: Whole black peppercorns are ground using either a molcajete (page 15) or a spice grinder. Using freshly ground pepper is the best choice when making Mexican food, but you can also use ground pepper.

.CILANTRO (fresh): Cilantro is used as an ingredient in salsas and stews, as well as a garnish for many dishes. To keep it fresh longer, wrap it in aluminum foil and place inside a plastic bag in your refrigerator.

CUMIN: You can use ground cumin or grind your own seeds at home (freshly ground is better) in a molcajete (page 15) or spice grinder.

EPAZOTE (fresh): Epazote is commonly used when cooking black beans. It is also used for some stews and corn-tortilla quesadillas, as well as in chilaquiles. If you can't find fresh epazote, you can find the dried leaves online. They won't have the same pungent taste epazote is known for, but they will still work.

PARSLEY (fresh): Parsley is used for garnishing many dishes. It is also used as an ingredient in some soups.

THYME (dried): Dried thyme is added to stews, main dishes, and pickled vegetables and peppers.

MEXICAN CINNAMON (sticks): Cinnamon has many uses in Mexican cuisine, from desserts and drinks to even some stews. It's always good to keep some in your pantry. Mexican cinnamon sticks can be found in Latin markets and online.

MEXICAN OREGANO (dried): Make sure to use Mexican oregano when cooking Mexican dishes, as its taste is quite different from the Italian and Greek oreganos. You can find it at Latin stores, specialty stores, and online.

DRY INGREDIENTS

ALL-PURPOSE FLOUR: Always buy a good-quality all-purpose flour, in order to obtain better results when making Flour Tortillas (page 21) or baked goods.

BEANS: Although there are many varieties of beans in Mexico, black beans and pinto beans are the most popular. I always have both in my pantry, and recommend you do the same.

CHICKEN BOUILLON: Chicken bouillon, available in cubes and as a powder, is a common ingredient in Mexican homes. People mix it with water to use as a substitute for chicken broth in many recipes, including soups and stews. You can use this substitution for the recipes in this book.

CORN HUSKS: You will use many corn husks when making tamales. When buying corn husks, check them to make sure they look clean, are the same size, and are still soft (not too dry or crunchy).

CORN TORTILLAS: If you don't have time to make your own tortillas (page 19), look for those sold at Latin stores or tortilla factories (*tortillerias*). Store-bought tortillas can freeze well for a couple of months when wrapped tightly in a freezer bag.

FLOUR TORTILLAS: Flour tortillas are not an everyday fare in many regions of Mexico, as they are only popular in the northern states. Nowadays, you can find cooked flour tortillas at most grocery stores, but I prefer to make my own at home (page 21).

LONG-GRAIN WHITE RICE: Long-grain white rice has less starch content than medium-grain rice, rendering a fluffy rice that won't stick together.

MASA HARINA: Masa harina is the flour that is used to make tortillas and several other Mexican foods (*masa* means "dough" and *harina* means "flour"). To produce masa harina, corn is first cooked in limewater in a process called "nixtamalization," and then it is dried and ground into a fine powder. While masa harina is sometimes referred to as "corn flour," it is important to not confuse it with regular corn flour, which does not use nixtamalized corn and is generally not ground as fine as masa harina is. If you are looking to buy this flour, make sure that the package says "masa harina" on it. You can find masa harina sold in Latin stores, and nowadays, a lot of grocery stores in the United States carry it as well. The most common brand is Maseca.

MEXICAN CHOCOLATE TABLETS: These chocolate tablets are commonly sold in a box containing six round tablets, each weighing about 3.2 ounces (90 g). The most popular brand is Abuelita (by Nestlé), with the second most common brand being Ibarra. If you cannot source Mexican chocolate tablets in your supermarket, they're available online.

PILONCILLO: This raw sugar comes in a cone shape. When buying piloncillo (also called *panela*, but not to be confused with panela cheese), make sure to look for the pure version, which has a dark color. Some stores carry a look-alike version that is just plain sugar in a cone shape, lacking the flavor and nutrients of the real piloncillo.

DAIRY

MEXICAN CREMA: Mexican crema is mostly used as a topping, drizzled on tostadas, crispy tacos, enchiladas, and other *antojitos* (Mexican street food). These days, Mexican crema is available at most supermarkets.

QUESO COTIJA: Like Mexican crema, queso Cotija is commonly used to top enchiladas and other Mexican antojitos. It can be substituted with crumbled queso fresco, or as a last resort, with Parmesan cheese.

QUESO FRESCO: Usually sold in a round wheel either in a plastic pouch or plastic container, queso fresco is perfect to use crumbled over refried beans, enchiladas, and more. You can use feta cheese if you can't find queso fresco, just keep in mind that feta is a saltier cheese compared to queso fresco.

QUESO OAXACA: Queso Oaxaca is often used as a filling for foods like quesadillas, tamales, and stuffed poblano peppers. Fresh mozzarella cheese is a good substitute.

QUESO PANELA: The texture of queso panela is somewhat spongy, but not as crumbly as queso fresco. Besides being used as garnish for antojitos, queso panela is also serve diced in soups like Sopa de Tortilla (page 42) and Sopa de Fideo (page 35). If you can't find queso panela, you can use queso fresco instead.

CANNED GOODS

CHIPOTLE PEPPERS IN ADOBO SAUCE: Chipotle peppers in adobo sauce are used to add flavor to dishes like Tinga de Pollo (page 101) and Camarones en Chipotle (page 70). Generally, only 1 or 2 peppers are used in a recipe, so once you open a can, save the remaining peppers in a container in your fridge.

CONDENSED MILK: Condensed milk is a staple in Mexican homes, and is used in a variety of sweet foods, including iconic desserts like Pastel de Tres Leches (page 165) and Flan (page 158). It is also drizzled on fruits, like fresh strawberries and fried plantains, and mixed into drinks, like coffee and even Agua de Horchata (page 173).

EVAPORATED MILK: Evaporated milk can be used as a creamer for coffee, but it is mostly used as an ingredient in desserts. It is one of the "three milks" used in Pastel de Tres Leches (page 165).

MEDIA CREMA (table cream): Besides being used in desserts, media crema is often used as a component for creamy soups. It can also be used as a substitute for Mexican crema.

PICKLED JALAPEÑOS and CARROTS: Pickled jalapeños and carrots are often served as an accompaniment to meals like stews or sandwiches. Besides being sold in cans, they are also available in jars.

FATS

LARD: Lard is used to enhance the flavors of dishes like Asado de Puerco (page 66), and it is also a component of the dough for making tamales. Lard is sometimes incorporated into the dough for antojitos, which can also be fried in lard.

OLIVE OIL: Traditionally, Spanish olive oil was used for preparing Mexican dishes with Spanish influence, like Pollo a la Veracruzana (page 100). Nowadays, Italian olive oil is becoming more popular, and it is being used in a larger variety of dishes. It is also commonly used in salads.

SHORTENING: Shortening is mainly used for baking cookies, breads, and other pastries.

VEGETABLE OIL: Vegetable oil is an essential ingredient that is used in the kitchen almost every day. It is used for cooking rice, stews, and even the eggs for breakfast.

TOOLS & EQUIPMENT

All of the recipes in this book can be made with tools and equipment that you are already have in your kitchen, but if you find yourself increasingly cooking Mexican food, you may want to invest in some of these traditional kitchen items.

BEAN MASHER: There are two types of bean mashers: those made with wood and those made with metal. Wooden bean mashers have a flat surface for mashing the beans, while the metal ones have holes in them, similar to a potato masher. If you don't have a bean masher, you can use a potato masher or a glass with a thick, heavy bottom.

CAZUELA: A cazuela is a traditional Mexican clay pot. It is convenient to have cazuelas that have lids (especially with vent holes). I recommend you have a small cazuela (around 8 inches/20 cm) for cooking rice and a medium one (10 to 12 inches/25 to 20 cm) for making stews.

CLOTH NAPKINS or KITCHEN TOWELS: Cloth napkins or kitchen towels are used to wrap warm tortillas when they are placed inside a tortilla basket. They are also used for covering the doughs for flour or corn tortillas, so they stay fresh while the tortillas are being formed.

COMAL: A comal is a flat, round griddle. They are commonly used for making and reheating tortillas; for roasting and toasting seeds, peppers, and vegetables for salsas; and reheating certain foods, like tamales. Comales can be made of clay, cast iron, or steel, and also come in nonstick varieties. I commonly use a nonstick comal, but you can use whichever type you prefer.

FREEZER BAGS (large): Freezer bags are not only useful for storing extra tamales, empanadas, beans, and any leftovers in the freezer, but they are my personal choice for making Corn Tortillas (page 19) and Empanadas (pages 80 and 82). For this purpose, cut two 7 x 7-inch (18 x 18 cm) plastic sheets from one resealable freezer bag, and then place a dough ball between them before pressing in a tortilla press or with a glass pie dish.

MOLCAJETE: A molcajete is a special mortar (with its accompanying pestle) that is made of lava rock, which has a very coarse, porous surface. Molcajetes are used for grinding spices, as well as for making and serving salsas and guacamole.

ROLLING PIN: In Mexican cuisine, rolling pins are mostly used for making Flour Tortillas (page 21). Due to their gluten content, flour tortillas cannot be made in a tortilla press and need to be rolled out using a rolling pin. Additionally, rolling pins are used for making cookies and pie crusts.

TAMALERA: A tamalera is a large pot with a steam rack at the bottom. As its name implies, it is used to cook tamales, but it can also be used to make certain steamed meats. If you're making tamales and don't have a tamalera, you can improvise one by using one of these methods: You can crumble up some aluminum foil and place it at the bottom of the pot, then cover it with corn husks and place the tamales on top, or you can cut some holes in a disposable aluminum pie dish, and then place it upside down in the pot to use as a steaming rack.

TORTILLA BASKET: The tortilla basket is a common sight in many Mexican households. They are made with natural fibers and are used to keep tortillas (wrapped in cloth napkins) warm at the table.

TORTILLA PRESS: Tortilla presses are used for making Corn Tortillas (page 19) and other foods that use masa harina, like empanadas, gorditas, and sopes. Tortilla presses are traditionally made of wood or cast iron, but are being made of other materials these days. In case you don't have access to a tortilla press, a very effective method I recommend is using a glass pie dish. You would need the same sheets of plastic you use with a tortilla press, but instead you would place the ball of dough between your work surface and the bottom of the pie dish. A benefit of doing it this way is that you can see the tortilla being formed through the glass as you press down on the pie dish, so you can make sure it has reached the desired diameter.

WOODEN SPOONS: Wooden spoons are among the utensils I use the most in my kitchen. They can be used when making stews, beans, and rice. Because they are wooden, they help protect your pots and pans from being scratched or damaged.

Roasted vegetables add a depth of flavor to salsas and sauces. Here's a quick guide to roasting vegetables for the recipes in this book.

ROASTING VEGETABLES

ANCHO/GUAJILLO PEPPERS: Clean the peppers with a damp kitchen cloth. Cut a slit along the length of the peppers using a knife or kitchen scissors, then remove the seeds and veins. Place the peppers open wide on a hot griddle or comal over medium-high heat and slightly roast them for 30 to 40 seconds. If needed, use a spatula to press them down. The peppers will release their aroma when they are ready. Remove promptly.

ÁRBOL PEPPERS: Place the peppers on a hot comal or skillet over medium-high heat and turn them 2 to 3 times until they start releasing their aroma and their skins change to a lighter color, 20 to 30 seconds. Remove promptly.

GARLIC: Keeping the peel on, place the cloves on a hot comal or skillet over medium-high heat for about 1 minute, turning them 2 or 3 times to roast evenly. The peel will be charred. Remove promptly. Peel the garlic before use.

ONIONS: Place the onion slices or quarters on a hot comal or skillet over medium-high heat for about 1 minute, turning them once. They will look charred and the texture will be slightly softened. Remove promptly.

POBLANO PEPPERS: Place the peppers over an open flame on your stove over medium-high heat for 5 to 6 minutes, turning them with kitchen tongs to roast evenly. The peppers will have charred skin all over and look slightly soft. After roasting, place the peppers in a plastic bag and close it to steam them for 5 minutes. This process makes the skins of the peppers loosen up for easy removal. Remove the peppers from the bag and scrape off the charred skins by rubbing your fingers on the surface of the pepper or using the edge of a spoon. You can leave some of the charred skins on, if you like, to add more flavor to the dish. Do not rinse the peppers, as they will lose some

of their flavor. With a sharp knife, cut a slit along the length of the peppers, then remove the seeds and veins. Alternatively, you can place them on a hot comal or skillet over medium-high heat for 8 to 10 minutes, turning them to roast evenly, or place them on a baking sheet under your broiler at 400°F (205°C) for 2 minutes, turning them once. An outdoor gas or charcoal grill can also be used. After roasting, continue with the steaming process.

SERRANO/JALAPEÑO PEPPERS: Place the peppers on a hot comal or skillet over medium-high heat for 5 minutes for serrano peppers and 7 to 8 minutes for jalapeños, turning them every 2 minutes or so to roast evenly. Their skins will have a semisoft texture.

TOMATILLOS: Place the tomatillos on a hot comal or skillet over medium-high heat for 6 minutes, turning them every 2 minutes or so to evenly roast. They will have a very soft texture.

TOMATOES: Place the tomatoes on a hot comal or skillet over medium-high heat for 8 minutes, turning them every 2 minutes or so to roast evenly. They will look charred all over and have a semisoft texture. They should be semi-cooked. For a large tomato that still looks raw after roasting, wrap it in a piece of foil for about 5 minutes to finish cooking in its steam.

CORN TORTILLAS

It goes without saying that corn tortillas are among the most quintessential food items in Mexican cuisine. In Mexico, tortillas are consumed during breakfast, lunch, and dinner. Besides being used for making tacos, tortillas are also very useful as a sort of utensil, used to scoop up sauces, stews, refried beans, scrambled eggs, and other foods. Corn tortillas are also great for dipping in soups, salsas, moles, and even egg yolks. These are all examples of the versatility of the tortilla, and why it continues to be an invaluable element of Mexican cuisine.

PREP TIME: 10 minutes	**COOK TIME:** 20 minutes	**YIELD:** 12 tortillas

1½ cups (150 g) masa harina

1¼ cups (300 ml) warm water, plus more if needed

1. Place the masa harina in a large bowl, then add the water, a little at a time. Using your hands, mix well until the water is evenly absorbed and the dough can be formed into a ball. Make sure you knead the dough well until it has a uniform texture.

2. Preheat a comal or large skillet over medium-high heat. This needs to be ready to go for when you start pressing the tortillas.

3. Grab a piece of the kneaded dough and form a golf ball–size ball with it, about 1½ inches (4 cm) in diameter. Place the dough ball, slightly flattened, between two plastic sheets made from a freezer bag. Using a tortilla press or a heavy glass pie dish, press down on the ball to form a round tortilla that is no more than ⅛ inch (3 mm) thick and 6 inches (15 cm) in diameter.

4. Open the tortilla press, then peel the top plastic sheet off. Lift the tortilla from the tortilla press, holding the bottom side. If the dough is too dry, the edges of your tortilla will look cracked, and you will need to add a little more water to the dough (see Notas on page 20) and knead it again.

5. To remove the bottom sheet of plastic, move the tortilla to your other hand so that the plastic sheet is facing up, then carefully peel off the sheet (this might take some practice). If the dough sticks to the plastic sheet and the tortilla doesn't stay intact, this means that the dough could be a little too wet. Add some more masa harina, 1 to 2 tablespoons (7 to 14 g), to the dough and mix again until it becomes easy to handle.

(continued)

6. Place the tortilla on the comal and cook for about 30 to 40 seconds. The edges of the tortilla will begin to dry out. Flip the tortilla over and continue to cook for another 40 to 45 seconds, until brown spots form on the bottom. The cooking time will vary depending on how thick your tortilla is and the temperature of your comal. Flip the tortilla over one last time and cook for another 15 seconds, until the tortilla begins to puff up. Lightly press down on the tortilla with your fingertips so that it puffs up evenly. The total cooking time is around 1 minute and 45 seconds.

7. Once the tortilla is cooked, wrap it in a cloth napkin or kitchen towel to serve. Continue forming and cooking the rest of the tortillas, and then placing them in the cloth napkin with the other tortillas. The wrapped tortillas will stay warm longer when placed in a tortilla basket made with natural fibers.

NOTAS

* *Traditionally, salt is not added to the corn dough for making tortillas. This is a personal choice, so you can add it if you like.*

* *The amount of water needed to make the dough will vary, depending on the humidity and other weather conditions. Have a couple extra tablespoons (30 ml) of water on hand to add to the dough if needed.*

* *When making the corn dough, it should have a soft consistency, and it should not stick to your hands. If it does, add a little more masa harina. If it looks dry or crumbly, add more water.*

* *You technically do not need a tortilla press to make tortillas, as many women in Mexico and Central America shape their tortillas by hand. However, this takes significant practice, and it is difficult to make the tortillas as thin as when using a press.*

* *While you're forming the tortillas, cover the dough with a moistened towel, in order to prevent it from drying.*

* *Fresh tortillas can be refrigerated for up to 4 days in a plastic bag or frozen for up to 2 months when stored in a tightly sealed freezer bag.*

* *To reheat, place a tortilla on a hot comal over medium-high heat and warm for 30 to 40 seconds per side. If the tortillas are frozen, thaw first before reheating.*

FLOUR TORTILLAS

Flour tortillas are more commonly found in the northern states of Mexico. For decades, the people there have faithfully used a traditional recipe that calls for 1 kilogram (2.2 pounds) of flour, ¼ kilogram (½ pound/250 g) of shortening, a pinch of salt, and hot water as needed. These amounts are so well known, stores sell flour in a 1-kilogram bag and shortening in a ¼-kilogram package. Today, people don't make flour tortillas at home as often as before, since you can find them at many stores as well as in *tortillerias*. Nevertheless, nothing beats a freshly made flour tortilla! My version of the recipe is designed for a smaller yield but has the same delicious flavor.

PREP TIME: 20 minutes plus 30 minutes resting time	**COOK TIME:** 10 minutes	**YIELD:** 10 large flour tortillas

2½ cups (325 g) all-purpose flour, plus more for the work surface and kneading

1 teaspoon salt

⅓ cup (80 g) shortening or lard

1 cup (240 ml) hot water

1. Place the flour and salt in a large bowl and mix together. With the help of a fork or pastry blender, or with your hands, incorporate the shortening until the mixture resembles a coarse meal.

2. Slowly add the hot water, a little at a time, until the dough starts to hold together. Do not add all the water at once (see Notas on page 23).

3. Transfer the dough to a lightly floured work surface (do not use too much flour or the tortillas will be dry) and knead for a couple of minutes, until it has a smooth texture.

4. Divide the dough into 10 equal-size pieces. Roll each piece on your work surface with the palm of your hand to form it into a ball. These balls of dough are called *testales*.

5. Place the testales on your work surface, a baking sheet, or in a large bowl and cover them with a damp kitchen towel or plastic wrap. Set them aside to rest for 30 to 45 minutes.

6. After the resting period, preheat a comal or large skillet over medium-high heat. Lightly flour your work surface and a rolling pin (do not use too much flour or the tortillas will be dry).

(continued)

7. To form the tortillas, place a testal on your work surface and slightly press it down with your hand. Place the rolling pin over the center of the testal and gently press forward and then backward (without making it to the edges). Turn the piece of dough 90 degrees (a half turn) and repeat this forward-and-backward pressing motion. Flip the dough again and repeat this process until you have formed a thin tortilla that is about 10 inches (25 cm) in diameter. (If you are new to rolling tortillas, be patient, it takes a little bit of practice.)

8. Once your tortilla has been formed, place it on the hot comal. The following steps happen quickly, so it's important to stay alert. During the first 20 to 30 seconds, the tortilla will form air bubbles and light brown spots will begin to show on the bottom side of the tortilla. At this point, turn the tortilla over for the first time. During the next 20 seconds, more air bubbles will continue to form. Flip the tortilla a second time. In the next 10 seconds, it should puff up and then deflate back to its normal size. The tortilla is now done.

9. Once the tortilla is cooked, wrap it in a cloth napkin or kitchen towel to keep it warm. Continue forming and cooking the rest of the tortillas, and then placing them in the cloth napkin with the other tortillas. The wrapped tortillas will stay warm longer when placed in a tortilla basket made with natural fibers.

NOTAS

* *Add ½ teaspoon of baking powder to the ingredients if you live at a high altitude. You can still make the tortillas without using the baking powder, but they will not puff up as much when cooking them (they will still turn out fine).*

* *Add the water, a little at a time, when forming the dough. In humid climates, the dough will require slightly less water, so it's important to be mindful of this.*

* *The resting period allows the gluten to develop, and this makes the dough easier to stretch when forming the tortillas. Do not skip this step (otherwise the dough will shrink back when stretched).*

* *The comal should be just hot enough, so when cooking the tortillas, the spots that form are a light-brown color. If the spots turn dark brown too quickly, then the heat is too high; if the tortilla takes longer to cook, then the heat is too low.*

* *Fresh tortillas can be refrigerated for up to 5 days in a plastic bag.*

* *To reheat, place a tortilla on a hot comal over medium-high heat and warm it the same way you cooked them in step 8, turning them twice. The air bubbles will form again, but they won't be as big as when the tortillas were cooked the first time.*

SOUPS

CALDO DE POLLO

Chicken Soup

Chicken soup is a dish that needs no introduction. Many cultures enjoy this comforting soup, and in Mexico, just like in other countries, it is often made when someone is feeling ill, or when you want a cozy meal to warm you up in the winter. This soup can be customized to the cook's liking, adding whatever vegetables they prefer or are available.

PREP TIME: 10 minutes	**COOK TIME:** 50 minutes	**YIELD:** 8 servings

1 whole chicken (about 3 to 4 pounds/ 1.4 to 1.8 kg), cut into pieces

3 quarts (2.8 L) water

2 teaspoons salt

½ white onion

4 cloves garlic

3 celery ribs

3 large carrots, peeled and diced

2 sprigs fresh cilantro

2 large white potatoes, peeled and diced

GARNISHING AND TO SERVE (OPTIONAL)

Arroz Blanco (page 130)

1 ripe avocado, halved, pitted, and diced

½ white onion, finely chopped

1 lime, cut into wedges

1 serrano or jalapeño pepper, diced

¼ cup (10 g) chopped fresh cilantro

Warm corn tortillas

1. Place the chicken, water, salt, onion, garlic, and celery in a large stockpot over medium-high heat. Bring to a boil, then use a large spoon to skim off any foam that forms on the surface. Partially cover the pot with the lid, reduce the heat, and gently simmer for about 30 minutes. Do not boil.

2. After the 30 minutes, check the chicken for doneness, then remove it from the pot and set aside (if it's not done yet, cook for 5 to 10 more minutes). After removing the chicken, add the carrots and cilantro to the pot, and continue cooking for 5 minutes.

3. Add the potatoes to the broth and simmer for 10 more minutes, or until the carrots and potatoes are completely cooked.

4. Once the chicken has cooled, shred it or cut it into bite-size pieces. Remove the potatoes and carrots from the pot and set aside.

5. Strain the broth using a strainer. Return the broth to the pot and let it settle for 8 to 10 minutes, removing the fat that rises to the surface with a large spoon.

6. Turn the heat to low to warm up the broth. Taste to check if it needs more salt. When ready to serve, place some cooked rice (if using) in a medium bowl, then a portion of the shredded chicken, the carrots and potatoes, and then stir in the warm broth. Let everyone garnish their own bowls of soup.

NOTA *You can add other vegetables to your soup, like zucchini, chayote, and green beans. Add these 5 minutes after you add the potatoes in step 3.*

CALDO DE RES

Beef and Vegetable Soup

This beef and vegetable soup is known in Mexico by many names, including *caldo*, *cocido*, and *puchero*. It is one of the many dishes Mexicans inherited from Spain and adapted to use with their local ingredients. The good thing about this soup is that many variations are possible, from simple to sophisticated. You can make this soup using your favorite selection of herbs, vegetables, and cuts of meat.

PREP TIME: 20 minutes	**COOK TIME:** 2 hours 30 minutes	**YIELD:** 6 servings

BROTH

2 pounds (900 g) bone-in beef shank

1½ pounds (675 g) beef marrow bones

2 ears corn, cut into thirds or quarters

3 halves medium white onions

4 cloves garlic

2 sprigs fresh mint

6 sprigs fresh cilantro

2 large carrots, peeled and sliced ½ inch (1 cm) thick

1 large chayote, peeled, pit removed, and cubed

2 small white potatoes, peeled and cubed

½ pound (225 g) green beans, trimmed and cut in half

2 small Mexican squash or zucchini, sliced ½ inch (1 cm) thick

⅓ head green cabbage, cubed

1 large plantain, sliced 1½ inches (4 cm) thick (optional)

2 cups (280 g) cooked garbanzo beans or 1 can (15 to 15.5 ounces/425 to 439 g), drained (optional)

Salt, to taste

1. To make the broth: Place the meat and bones in a large stockpot, along with the corn, onion, garlic, mint, and cilantro. If you prefer, you can tie the herbs together. Add enough water to cover the ingredients, then turn the heat to low. Simmer for about 2 hours, or until the meat is tender. Using a large spoon, skim off any foam that forms on the surface.

2. To make the tomato sauce (optional): Place all the sauce ingredients in a blender and blend until smooth. This sauce will be added to the broth along with the vegetables.

3. Increase the heat to bring the broth back to a simmering point. Add the carrots and chayote, and cook for about 15 minutes. Add the potatoes and cook for 10 more minutes, making sure all the vegetables are still al dente. Add the remaining vegetables, tomato sauce (if using), garbanzo beans (if using), and salt, and let the broth simmer until all the vegetables are cooked, about 10 more minutes. It is important to cook the vegetables in stages to avoid overcooking them.

4. Serve the soup in large bowls and garnish with the cilantro. Serve with the corn tortillas, lime wedges, and serrano pepper (if using).

TOMATO SAUCE (optional)

2 medium tomatoes, chopped

2 cloves garlic, chopped

¼ cup (30 g) chopped white onion

¼ cup (60 ml) water

GARNISHING AND TO SERVE

Chopped fresh cilantro

Warm corn tortillas

1 lime, cut into wedges

1 serrano pepper, finely chopped (optional)

NOTAS

* *Other cuts of meat you can use are beef short ribs and beef chuck cut into large cubes.*

* *I usually cook the meat in a pressure cooker or Instant Pot first for 35 minutes, then remove the meat and the broth (with the foam skimmed off). Doing this will save you a lot of time.*

* *In some regions of Mexico, cooks add the tomato sauce to the broth (this is the way I grew up eating this soup). You can skip this if you like; either way, it will turn out delicious.*

CREMA DE ELOTE

Cream of Corn Soup

This corn soup is a tasty and soul-warming comfort food. With its thick, creamy texture, it's bound to win over the whole family, even the kids. My son has loved this soup ever since he was a little boy. If you're making this soup in the winter when you can't find fresh corn, you can use frozen or canned corn.

PREP TIME: 10 minutes	**COOK TIME:** 25 minutes	**YIELD:** 4 servings

2 tablespoons (30 g) butter

⅓ cup (40 g) finely chopped white onion

2 cloves garlic, chopped

About 5 ears corn (2½ to 3 pounds/ 1.1 to 1.4 kg), kernels removed from the cob, or 1 package (10 ounces/ 283 g) frozen corn, thawed, or 1 can (15 to 15.5 ounces/425 to 439 g) corn, drained

2 cups (480 ml) chicken broth

1 tablespoon (8.5 g) all-purpose flour

2 cups (480 ml) milk

Salt and pepper, to taste

GARNISHING AND TO SERVE

1 poblano pepper, roasted, seeded, veins removed, and finely chopped (optional)

½ cup (80 g) cubed queso fresco, panela cheese, or farmer cheese

Squash blossoms (optional)

¼ cup (60 g) Mexican crema or heavy cream (optional)

1. Melt the butter in a medium saucepan over medium-low heat. Add the onion and garlic, and cook for about 5 minutes, until they are softened but not browned, regularly stirring to keep from sticking to the bottom of the pan.

2. Increase the heat to medium-high, then add the corn kernels and chicken broth. Bring to a simmer, then reduce the heat to medium-low and gently simmer for 15 minutes, or until the corn is tender. Remove about ½ cup (80 g) of the kernels with a slotted spoon and reserve for garnishing.

3. While the soup simmers, whisk the flour with the milk in a small bowl, mixing well to dissolve any lumps.

4. Place the milk and flour mixture into a blender and add the broth with the cooked corn. Blend until smooth. Return the puréed soup to the saucepan and simmer over medium heat until it's hot and the soup has thickened, about 5 more minutes. Stir the soup to keep it from sticking to the pan. It should have a thick consistency. Season with the salt and pepper.

5. Serve the soup in medium bowls, garnished with the poblano pepper (if using), reserved corn kernels, cheese cubes, and squash blossoms (if using). Drizzle with the Mexican crema (if using).

NOTA *The thickness of the soup will depend not only on the amount of flour, but also on the natural starch content of the corn; some corn has higher amounts of starch than others. For a thicker consistency, add an extra tablespoon (8.5 g) flour.*

CREMA DE PAPA

Cream of Potato Soup

When I was growing up, my mother was an expert at stretching the kitchen budget. She would always add vegetables and other ingredients to her dishes in order to increase their yield. She used a lot of potatoes because she knew that her kids loved them, and because of this, potatoes became an essential part of many of the dishes she made, like this soup. She served this soup with hot dogs or sausages cut into little pieces to delight her children.

PREP TIME: 10 minutes	**COOK TIME:** 30 minutes	**YIELD:** 4 servings

1 pound (450 g) white potatoes (about 3 medium potatoes), peeled and cut in half

2 cups (480 ml) whole milk, plus more if needed

2 cups (480 ml) chicken broth, plus more if needed

2 tablespoons (30 g) butter

⅓ cup (40 g) finely chopped white onion

1 clove garlic, minced

1 tablespoon (8.5 g) all-purpose flour

Salt and pepper, to taste

GARNISHING AND TO SERVE

Chopped fresh parsley

2 slices bacon, cooked and chopped into pieces

1. Place the potatoes in a saucepan and cover with water. Cook over medium-high heat for 18 to 20 minutes, or until they're soft.

2. Drain the potatoes and place them in a blender with the milk and chicken broth. Blend until creamy and smooth. Set aside.

3. In the same saucepan you cooked the potatoes, melt the butter over low heat, then add the onion and garlic, and cook until the onion is transparent, about 2 minutes. Stir in the flour and cook for another minute. Use a wooden spoon to dissolve any lumps.

4. Pour the creamy potato mixture into the saucepan and turn the heat to medium-high. Once it starts boiling, reduce the heat to low and simmer for about 8 minutes, stirring frequently to prevent the soup from sticking to the bottom of the pan. Season with the salt and pepper. If you prefer your soup with a thinner consistency, add more milk or chicken broth.

5. Serve the soup in medium bowls and garnish with the parsley and bacon pieces.

NOTAS

✖ *You can use other types of potatoes to make this soup.*

✖ *You can substitute leek, yellow onion, or scallion for the white onion.*

SOPA DE LENTEJAS

Lentil Soup

Lentil soup has many variations throughout Mexico, and depending on the region of the country, you can find it made with ingredients such as chorizo, pork, and bacon. I like to add diced carrots to my lentil soup, but many cooks add fried plantains and sliced hard-boiled eggs. You can also find this soup prepared with a simple tomato base or with an adobo-type-sauce base that includes tomatoes, garlic, onion, and ancho peppers.

PREP TIME: 5 minutes	**COOK TIME:** 30 minutes	**YIELD:** 6 servings

2 tablespoons (30 ml) olive oil

½ cup (60 g) finely chopped white onion

1 large clove garlic, minced

1½ cups (200 g) finely chopped celery (2 large ribs)

⅔ cup (100 g) diced carrot

½ pound (225 g) lentils (about 1¼ cups), well washed and drained

6 cups (1½ quarts/1.4 L) chicken broth

2 sprigs fresh parsley, finely chopped

Salt and pepper, to taste

Lime wedges, to serve

1. Heat the olive oil in a large saucepan over medium heat. Add the onion and garlic, and cook for 5 minutes.

2. Reduce the heat to low, add the celery and carrots, and cook for 10 minutes. Stir in the drained lentils, chicken broth, and parsley. Increase the heat to medium-high and bring to a boil.

3. Reduce the heat to a simmer and cook for 25 to 30 minutes (cooking time may vary depending on the type of lentils and how old they are). Season the soup with the salt and pepper.

4. Serve the soup in medium bowls, adding a few drops of lime juice from the lime wedges.

NOTA *Homemade chicken broth is the best option for making this soup, but you can substitute it with 6 cups (1½ quarts/1.4 L) water and 2 chicken bouillon cubes.*

SOPA DE FIDEO

Mexican Noodle Soup

Sopa de fideo is one of the most traditional soups in Mexico, and is usually part of the midday meal in households and in small family restaurants called *fondas*. As a kid, I loved coming home from school and finding that my mom had made this soup. It is one of the easiest meals to make, and the kids love it. It's a must-have lunchtime soup in every Mexican home.

PREP TIME: 15 minutes	**COOK TIME:** 16 minutes	**YIELD:** 4 servings

10 ounces (280 g) fresh plum tomatoes, chopped

1 large clove garlic or 2 small cloves, chopped

½ cup (60 g) chopped white onion

2 tablespoons (30 ml) vegetable oil

8 ounces (225 g) vermicelli pasta (fideo noodles)

6 cups (1½ quarts/1.4 L) chicken or vegetable broth

Salt and pepper, to taste

GARNISHING AND TO SERVE

Crumbled queso fresco

Diced avocado

1. Place the tomatoes, garlic, and onion in a blender, and blend until smooth. Using a colander, strain this mixture into a bowl and set aside.

2. Heat the oil in a large saucepan over medium-low heat, and add the fideo noodles. Slightly fry the noodles, stirring often, until they have a light golden-brown color, 3 to 4 minutes.

3. Pour the tomato mixture into the saucepan and cook for about 1 minute. Stir in the chicken broth and bring to a boil. Reduce the heat to medium-low and simmer, covered, until the noodles are tender, about 8 minutes. Don't overcook the noodles. Season the soup with the salt and pepper.

4. Serve the soup in bowls and garnish with the queso fresco and diced avocado.

NOTAS

* *Roasting the tomatoes first will add an even deeper flavor to the soup. See page 16 for roasting instructions.*
* *You can add diced vegetables, like peas and carrots, in step 3 after you add the chicken broth.*

MENUDO

Mexican Tripe Soup

Menudo, *pancita*, and *mondongo* are some of the names that this soup is known by in Mexico. It's famous for its taste and aroma, as well as for the distinctively spongy texture of the tripe. Commonly regarded as an excellent cure for a hangover, many people swear by this soup's ability to bring them back to life after a long night out. Menudo is usually sold on the weekends at markets and at small mom-and-pop eateries known as *fondas*, or at restaurants that specialize in typical Mexican *antojitos* (street food).

PREP TIME: 10 minutes	COOK TIME: 2 hours 30 minutes	YIELD: 8 servings

BROTH

6 quarts (5.7 L) water

1 cow's foot (usually sold already cut into pieces)

1 pound (450 g) beef marrow bones

4 large cloves garlic

1 medium white onion, cut into thick slices

Salt, to taste

3 pounds (1.4 kg) clean honeycomb tripe, cut into bite-size pieces

2 teaspoons dried Mexican oregano

GUAJILLO SAUCE

6 guajillo peppers, sliced open, seeded, and veins removed

3 cloves garlic

1 teaspoon freshly ground cumin seeds (optional)

GARNISHING AND TO SERVE

1 tablespoon (5 g) crushed dried piquín peppers

Limes, cut into wedges

Dried Mexican oregano

¾ cup (90 g) finely chopped white onion

Warm corn tortillas

1. To make the broth: Add the water, cow's foot, marrow bones, garlic, and onion to a large stockpot over medium heat. Season with the salt. Bring to a simmer, uncovered, and cook for about 15 minutes. While it cooks, use a spoon to skim off any foam that forms on the surface.

2. Add the tripe and oregano, and cook for 2 to 2 ½ hours, until the tripe is tender but firm (do not overcook it).

3. Remove the cow's foot and marrow bones from the pot and skim off the fat that has formed on the surface. Once the cow's foot cools a little, remove the bones, chop up the meaty parts, and return them to the pot, along with the marrow from the bones (but not the bones).

4. While the broth is cooking, make the guajillo sauce: Preheat a comal or large skillet over medium-high heat, then place the guajillo peppers open wide in the pan and lightly roast them for 30 to 40 seconds. Remove promptly. Place the roasted peppers in a bowl and cover them with water. Let them soak for about 25 minutes until soft. Drain the peppers and place them in a blender with the garlic, ½ cup (120 g) of the cooking broth, and cumin (if using). Blend until smooth. Strain the sauce through a strainer and pour it into the pot with the broth.

5. Simmer the broth for another 30 minutes, partially covered. Taste and season with more salt if needed.

6. Serve the soup in large bowls and place the garnishes in serving dishes for everyone to add to their own bowls.

NOTAS

* *If using an Instant Pot, cook the ingredients in step 2 for 30 minutes. If using a pressure cooker, cook for 45 minutes. You can also use a slow cooker, cooking for 6 hours on the low setting.*

* *If you want your broth to have a darker color, add 2 ancho peppers (in addition to the guajillo peppers) to the sauce. Prepare them the same way as the guajillo peppers in step 4.*

* *Some people like to add hominy to their menudo. If you can buy hominy in a can, drain it and add it to the soup during the final simmering in step 5.*

POZOLE ROJO

Red Pozole

Red pozole is one of those dishes that tastes even better when you reheat it the next day. This is a meal that is usually prepared for birthdays, holidays, and other special occasions. It is common to find it sold at *cenadurías*, restaurants where typical Mexican dishes are sold. There are many types of pozole, including green (page 40) and white variations, and some are even made with chicken and shrimp. Nevertheless, red pozole is the all-time favorite.

PREP TIME: 15 minutes	**COOK TIME:** 2 hour 45 minutes	**YIELD:** 8 servings

SOUP

4 quarts (3.8 L) water

2 pounds (900 g) pork shoulder, cut into cubes

1 pound (450 g) pork spare ribs or baby back ribs

1 white onion, cut into quarters

8 large cloves garlic

Salt and pepper, to taste

3 cans (15 to 15.5 ounces/425 to 439 g each) white hominy, drained and rinsed

RED SAUCE

5 guajillo peppers, sliced open, seeded, and veins removed

5 ancho peppers, sliced open, seeded, and veins removed

6 cloves garlic

1 medium white onion, coarsely chopped

½ teaspoon dried Mexican oregano

2 tablespoons (30 ml) vegetable or canola oil

Salt, to taste

1. To make the soup: Add the water, pork shoulder, spare ribs, onion, and garlic to a large stockpot over medium-high heat. Bring to a boil, then reduce the heat to low and let simmer, partially covered, for 2½ hours, or until the meat is tender and falling off the bones. Season with the salt when the meat is almost done cooking. While cooking, use a ladle or slotted spoon to skim off the foam that forms on the surface.

2. Remove the pork shoulder and spare ribs from the pot, trim any excess fat, and remove any bones. Remove and discard the garlic and onion from the broth. Strain the broth and return it to the pot. Shred the pork with two forks and return it to the pot.

3. While the pork cooks, make the red sauce: Soak the guajillo and ancho peppers in just enough water to cover them for 25 to 30 minutes until they are soft.

4. Add the peppers, garlic, onion, and oregano to a blender, along with about 1 cup (240 ml) of the cooking broth or water. Blend until smooth.

5. Heat the oil in a large skillet over medium-high heat and add the sauce and salt. Constantly stir the mixture, being careful as it may splatter. Reduce the heat to medium, then simmer for about 25 minutes.

6. Using a strainer, add the sauce to the broth. Increase the heat to medium-high and bring to a boil. Reduce the heat, cover, and gently simmer for about 10 minutes. Stir in the white hominy and season with salt and pepper. Simmer until all the ingredients are heated through.

GARNISHING AND TO SERVE

1 head iceberg lettuce, finely shredded

1½ cups (175 g) finely chopped white onion

Crushed dried piquín peppers

1 bunch radishes, thinly sliced

Dried Mexican oregano

Corn tostadas

Limes, cut in wedges

Diced avocado

7. Serve the pozole in large Mexican soup bowls and place the garnishes in serving dishes for everyone to add to their own bowls.

NOTA *Pozole is traditionally made using parts of the pig's head, as they add a lot of flavor, but you can use other cuts of pork that contain bones and fat to achieve similar results.*

POZOLE VERDE DE POLLO

Green Pozole with Chicken

While the most popular pozole in Mexico is Pozole Rojo (page 38), there are also green and white pozoles. All pozoles are usually made with pork, but green pozole can also be made with chicken, like in this recipe. This recipe is similar in style to the one found in the state of Guerrero and was given to me some years ago by my dear friend Nora. Long before I started blogging, we used to email each other to talk and exchange recipes and photos of our cooking. I've made a few changes to the recipe, but I know she would be glad that I included it in this book.

PREP TIME: 20 minutes	**COOK TIME:** 50 minutes	**YIELD:** 8 servings

BROTH

4 skin-on chicken thighs and legs and 2 large skin-on, bone-in chicken breasts

½ white onion

6 cloves garlic

2 sprigs fresh cilantro

Salt, to taste

2 cans (15 to 15.5 ounces/425 to 439 g each) white hominy, rinsed and drained

2 chicken bouillon cubes (optional)

GREEN SAUCE

⅓ cup (50 g) pumpkin seeds

2 poblano peppers, roasted, seeded, and veins removed (see page 16 for roasting instructions)

1 serrano or jalapeño pepper

1 pound (450 g) tomatillos (about 11 medium tomatillos), husks removed

2 cloves garlic

⅓ cup (13 g) chopped fresh cilantro

2 epazote leaves

6 to 8 radish leaves

¼ cup (30 g) finely chopped white onion

1. To make the broth: Place the chicken, onion, garlic, cilantro, and salt in a large stockpot. Fill the pot with enough water to cover the meat, place over medium-high heat, and bring to a boil. Reduce the heat and simmer until the chicken is cooked and soft enough to shred, 40 to 45 minutes.

2. Remove the chicken from the pot and remove and discard the skin and bones. Place the meat in a large bowl to cool. Shred the chicken or cut it into bite-size pieces. Strain the broth in which the chicken was cooked and discard the cilantro, garlic, and onion. Return the broth and the chicken to the pot, and add the white hominy.

3. While the chicken is cooking, make the green sauce: Lightly toast the pumpkin seeds in a hot skillet until they start "dancing" (popping), taking care not to burn them. Remove them from the skillet and let them cool.

4. Add the pumpkin seeds, peppers, tomatillos, garlic, cilantro, epazote, radish leaves, onion, oregano, cumin, and pepper (freshly ground, if possible), along with about 1½ cups (350 ml) of the chicken broth, to a blender. Blend until smooth.

5. In a large skillet, heat the vegetable oil. Add the sauce and cook until it changes to a darker color, about 7 minutes. Season with the salt, then reduce the temperature and continue cooking for about 1 more minute, stirring frequently.

½ teaspoon dried Mexican oregano

½ teaspoon freshly ground cumin seeds

Salt and pepper, to taste

2 tablespoons (30 ml) vegetable oil

GARNISHING AND TO SERVE

¼ head romaine (cos) or iceberg lettuce, finely shredded

½ cup (60 g) finely chopped white onion

2 limes, cut into wedges

8 radishes, thinly sliced

Crushed dried piquín peppers

Dried Mexican oregano

16 corn tostadas

6. Place the stockpot with the chicken, broth, and hominy over medium-high heat. When the soup reaches boiling point, pour the sauce into the pot, then reduce the heat and simmer for 6 to 7 more minutes. Taste the pozole to check if it needs extra seasoning. If you want, add the chicken bouillon to increase the flavor.

7. Serve the green pozole in large bowls and place the garnishes in serving dishes for everyone to add to their own bowls.

NOTA *You can also roast the tomatillos, garlic, and onion for the sauce. See page 16 for roasting instructions.*

SOPA DE TORTILLA

Tortilla Soup

Tortilla soup is one of the most famous soups from central Mexico. There are several variations to the recipe, and they can include shredded chicken, roasted poblano peppers, and even chicharrones. What makes this soup special (and famous!) are the garnishes; the combination of the crispy tortillas and the creamy avocado chunks make for a spoonful of heaven.

PREP TIME: 10 minutes	COOK TIME: 25 minutes	YIELD: 4 servings

2 medium tomatoes

2 cloves garlic, unpeeled

⅓ medium white onion

6 cups (1½ quarts/1.4 L) chicken broth, plus more if needed

5 tablespoons (75 ml) vegetable oil, divided

6 corn tortillas (day-old tortillas are best; see Notas)

1 sprig epazote (about 4 leaves)

Salt and pepper, to taste

1 or 2 pasilla peppers, sliced into rings

GARNISHING AND TO SERVE

1 ripe avocado, halved, pitted, and diced

1 cup (125 g) panela cheese, cut into small cubes

Mexican crema

Lime wedges

1½ cups (about 225 g) shredded cooked chicken (optional)

1 roasted poblano pepper, cut into strips (see page 16 for roasting instructions) (optional)

Chopped onion, to taste (optional)

Chopped fresh cilantro, to taste (optional)

1. Preheat a comal or large skillet over medium-high heat, then roast the tomatoes, garlic, and onion, turning them so they can roast evenly. (See page 16 for specific roasting instructions for each vegetable.) Once roasted, peel the tomatoes and garlic.

2. Place the roasted vegetables in a blender. Blend until smooth, adding about 1 cup (240 ml) chicken broth, if needed.

3. In a large saucepan, heat 1 tablespoon (15 ml) of the vegetable oil over medium-high heat. Add the tomato sauce and cook for about 3 minutes. When the sauce starts to boil, reduce the heat and simmer for 5 minutes. The sauce will reduce and change to a darker color.

4. While the sauce is cooking, cut the tortillas into thin strips that are 2 inches (5 cm) long and ½ inch (1 cm) wide. Set aside.

5. Add the chicken broth to the sauce, increase the heat to medium-high, and bring to a boil. Reduce the heat and simmer for 10 to 12 more minutes. Add the epazote and season with the salt and pepper. Simmer for 3 more minutes.

6. In a large skillet, heat the remaining 4 tablespoons (60 ml) oil and fry the tortilla strips until they are crispy and take on a golden color, about 4 minutes (fry them in batches so you don't overcrowd the skillet). Remove the fried tortillas with a slotted spoon and place them on a paper towel–lined plate to drain the excess oil.

7. In the remaining oil, fry the pasilla pepper rings. These will get crispy quickly. Once they do, immediately remove them and set aside.

8. Ladle the soup into medium bowls and top with the tortilla strips. Place the garnishes in serving dishes for everyone to add to their own bowls.

NOTAS

✖ *Some cooks prefer not to roast the tomato, onion, and garlic.*

✖ *You can also add a pasilla pepper to the sauce. Soak it in water until it softens, then add it with the other ingredients in the blender in step 2.*

✖ *Day-old tortillas are better for frying, since they are drier and absorb less oil. They also tend to get crispy faster. If you have fresh tortillas and want to dry them, cut them and leave them on your kitchen counter overnight, covered with a paper towel, or place them in the oven at 250°F (120°C) for 10 to 12 minutes before frying. You can also bake the tortilla strips instead of frying them, at 350°F (175°C) for 8 to 10 minutes.*

MAIN
DISHES

TACOS DE BISTEC

Steak Tacos

If I had to confess to one weakness, it would be tacos. I love them, especially the ones that are sold at *taquerias*, which contain only meat, a topping of fresh cilantro and chopped onion, and, in my case, a very spicy salsa. If you have visited Mexico, you have probably seen these taco stands at night, with the lights hanging from the roof and lots of people gathered around. This recipe for street-style steak tacos does not disappoint.

PREP TIME: 10 minutes	**COOK TIME:** 20 minutes	**YIELD:** 12 tacos

1 tablespoon lard (15 g) or vegetable oil (15 ml) (lard is better for an authentic taste), plus more if needed

2 pounds (900 g) thinly sliced rib-eye or chuck steaks

Salt, to taste

12 corn tortillas

1 medium white onion, finely chopped

1 bunch fresh cilantro, finely chopped

TO SERVE

Spicy salsa of your choice

NOTAS

✖ *In certain Latin markets, you may be able to find meat already sliced thinly.*

✖ *A variation of this dish is* tacos campechanos, *in which the chopped steak is mixed with chorizo. Simply fry up some chorizo in the same skillet you cooked the steaks, then warm it with the chopped steak in step 3.*

1. Add the lard to a large skillet over medium-high heat. Season the meat with the salt. Add the steaks to the skillet. Cook the steaks for about 2 minutes per side. If you are making several steaks, wrap the cooked ones in aluminum foil and keep them in a warm oven or near the heat while you finish cooking the remainder of the steaks. Make sure not to overcook them.

2. While the meat is cooking, start warming the tortillas in a separate large skillet over medium heat. Wrap the warmed tortillas in a cloth kitchen towel.

3. Once all the meat is partially cooked, chop it into pieces that are ⅓ inch (8 mm) or smaller, then return it to the skillet to warm it again. Stir the meat to ensure it thoroughly heats through. If you want, you can add an extra dab of lard (or drizzle of oil) to the skillet.

4. Assemble the tacos by placing a portion of the meat onto each warm tortilla. Some taco stands warm their tortillas in the same skillet as the meat; this way they absorb some of the flavor (some also add more oil or lard to the skillet while warming the tortillas). Top each taco with the chopped onion and cilantro.

5. Serve with the salsa.

FLAUTAS DE PAPA

Crispy Rolled Potato Tacos

Flautas de papa are rolled tacos that are filled with mashed potatoes and fried. Crispy on the outside, with a creamy filling inside, these flautas make a great meatless meal that everyone will love, especially the kids. I like to serve them topped with shredded lettuce or cabbage, sliced tomato, crumbled queso fresco, and a drizzle of Mexican crema.

PREP TIME: 15 minutes	**COOK TIME:** 30 minutes	**YIELD:** 6 servings

1¼ pounds (570 g) potatoes, unpeeled and left whole

Salt and pepper, to taste

½ cup (120 ml) vegetable oil, plus more if needed, to fry the tacos

12 corn tortillas

GARNISHING AND TO SERVE

2 cups (120 g) shredded green cabbage

⅓ cup (40 g) crumbled queso fresco or Cotija cheese

2 small tomatoes, sliced

¼ white onion, thinly sliced

1 ripe avocado, halved, pitted, and sliced (optional)

½ cup (120 ml) Mexican crema (optional)

Spicy salsa of your choice (optional)

1. Place the whole potatoes in a medium saucepan and cover with cold water. Do not peel or cut them; this prevents the potatoes from absorbing too much water, as any excess moisture will be released in the form of bubbles during the frying process, causing the oil to splatter. Turn the heat to medium-high and bring to a boil. Cook for 20 minutes, or until the potatoes are tender. Remove them from the pan and place them in a large bowl. Wait until they're cool enough to handle, then peel and discard the skins.

2. Season the potatoes with the salt and pepper, then mash them until you have a smooth paste (it won't look like a purée but more like a potato paste). Set aside.

3. Heat the oil in a large skillet over medium-high heat. While waiting for the oil to heat up, slightly warm the tortillas one by one on a hot comal or in a skillet; this will make them more pliable and easier to roll.

4. To assemble the flautas, place about 2 to 3 tablespoons (25 to 40 g) of the mashed potatoes (the amount needed will depend on the size of the tortilla) on a tortilla, close to one edge. Roll the tortilla tightly, but not so tight that the filling comes out. (You can use a toothpick to secure the flauta when frying.). Repeat this process with the remaining tortillas and filling.

5. Add the rolled flautas to the pan and cook them for about 2 minutes per side, until golden and crisp (fry them in batches so you don't overcrowd the pan). Remove the flautas and place them on a a paper towel–lined plate to drain the excess oil. Allow the flautas to cool a bit before serving, because the filling will be very hot when they come out of the oil.

6. To serve, garnish with the shredded cabbage, queso fresco, tomato, onion, avocado (if using), Mexican crema (if using), and salsa (if using).

NOTAS

✻ *For these tacos, I prefer to use red or Yukon Gold potatoes. I have found that russet potatoes absorb too much oil.*

✻ *If you like, you can mix queso fresco with the mashed potatoes to make cheesy potato flautas.*

✻ *These keep for up to 4 days in the refrigerator and up to 6 weeks in the freezer. To reheat, completely thaw and place on a hot comal until warmed, or warm in an oven at 350°F (175°C) for 15 minutes.*

CARNITAS

Some of the most succulent tacos you will ever eat are made with *carnitas*. This taco is a warm corn tortilla, filled with a mixture of tender and crispy morsels of pork, shining with pork fat drippings and topped with the obligatory chopped onion and fresh cilantro. Carnitas are made with various cuts of pork that are traditionally slow-cooked in copper cauldrons over an open fire. At dedicated carnitas shops, most parts of the pig will be used; some will be cooked until tender, juicy, and golden outside, while other parts will be cooked until crispy, just like chicharrones.

PREP TIME: 10 minutes	**COOK TIME:** 1 hour 5 minutes	**YIELD:** 6 servings

2 pounds (900 g) pork shoulder and pork butt, cut into 2-inch (5 cm) cubes

¼ cup lard (60 g) or vegetable oil (60 ml)

3 cloves garlic (optional)

1 tablespoon (15 g) salt

TO SERVE

Warm corn tortillas

Chopped white onion

Chopped fresh cilantro

Salsa Verde (page 125)

1. Place the pork, lard, and garlic (if using) in a large Dutch oven or cast-iron pot. Fill with enough water to cover the meat and then add the salt.

2. Cook, covered, over medium-high heat until the water comes to a boil, then reduce the heat and simmer for about 45 minutes, until the pork is almost tender.

3. Uncover the pot and increase the heat to medium-high to reduce the liquid. The meat will start frying in its own fat and lard at this point.

4. Reduce the heat to medium-low and carefully cook the meat, stirring frequently, until the pork is evenly browned, 15 to 20 minutes. Be careful not to overcook the meat or it will end up very dry.

5. Serve with the tortillas, onion, cilantro, and salsa for making tacos.

NOTAS

* *Pork shrinks a lot when you cook it, so consider doubling or tripling the amount if you want leftovers.*

* *If you do not have the time to watch the stove while the meat cooks, here is my recipe for oven-baked carnitas: Add the meat, lard, and salt, along with 1 cup (240 ml) water, to an oven bag and place it in a large baking pan. Cook in an oven preheated to 350°F (175°C) for 2 hours. Take the bag out of the oven to drain and discard most of the juices released by the meat, then close the bag and place it back in the oven for another hour or so, until the meat is golden brown.*

BARBACOA DE LENGUA

Beef Tongue Barbacoa Tacos

Barbacoa is derived from the word for "barbecue," and this is the easiest way to make beef tongue barbacoa in your home. The texture of the meat is soft and sort of creamy if well cooked, to the point that it almost melts in your mouth. The leftovers (if any) are great for making lots of things, including tortas and flautas.

PREP TIME: 5 minutes	COOK TIME: 8 hours	YIELD: 6 to 8 servings

1 beef tongue (2 to 3 pounds/ 900 to 1.4 kg)

¼ medium white onion

4 cloves garlic

1 bay leaf

Salt, to taste

GARNISHING AND TO SERVE

Warm corn tortillas

1 cup (40 g) chopped fresh cilantro

1 cup (115 g) chopped white onion

Salsa of your choice

1. Rinse the beef tongue with water and place it in a slow cooker. Add the onion, garlic, bay leaf, and salt, and enough water to cover the meat. Cover the pot and set it on low for 8 hours. Cook until tender. If after 8 hours the meat is not tender enough to shred, cook it a little longer.

2. Remove the beef tongue from the pot and place it on a large dish. Using a knife, make a cut along the length of the beef tongue, then peel and discard the skin. Trim off any fatty tissue at the back end of the tongue.

3. Shred the meat using two forks and place it in a serving bowl. Add about ½ cup (120 ml) of the cooking liquid (that has had the fat removed and been strained) to keep the meat moist.

4. Serve with the tortillas and place the garnishes in serving dishes for everyone to make their own tacos.

NOTAS

* To cook the beef tongue using an Instant Pot, prepare as directed and cook for 45 minutes on the pressure cooker setting. If using a stove-top pressure cooker, cook for 1 hour. If using a regular stockpot, cook the tongue for 2½ to 3 hours over medium-low heat.

* Any leftover barbacoa will keep for up to 2 days in the refrigerator or 1 month in the freezer.

CHILES RELLENOS

Chiles rellenos are peppers, usually poblanos, that are stuffed with a filling and then fried in an egg batter. The choice of fillings include meat, cheese, vegetables, tuna, shrimp, and mushrooms, just to mention a few. A very common filling is Picadillo (page 99), which is used in this recipe. Making this dish requires some time and skill in the kitchen, but it's worth it.

PREP TIME: 30 minutes	**COOK TIME:** 25 minutes	**YIELD:** 6 servings

SAUCE

20 ounces (570 g) plum tomatoes (about 4 tomatoes)

¼ whole plus ¼ cup (30 g) chopped medium white onion, divided

2 small cloves garlic

4 cups (1 quart/950 ml) water, plus more if needed

1 tablespoon (15 ml) vegetable oil

½ teaspoon salt

PEPPERS

6 medium poblano peppers

2½ cups (500 g) Picadillo (page 99)

1 cup (240 ml) vegetable oil, plus more if needed, for frying the stuffed chiles

4 large eggs, separated

¾ cup (100 g) all-purpose flour

½ teaspoon salt

TO SERVE

Arroz Blanco (page 130) or Arroz Rojo (page 132)

1. To make the sauce: Place the tomatoes, ¼ whole onion, and garlic in a large saucepan, and cover with water. Turn the heat to high, cover, and bring to a boil. Reduce the heat to a simmer and cook until the tomatoes are soft and the skins are peeling.

2. Carefully place the cooked tomatoes, onion, and garlic in a blender, and blend until smooth. Only add a few tablespoons (45 ml) of water if the blender is having a hard time processing the ingredients.

3. Heat the oil in a skillet over medium heat, then add the remaining chopped onion and cook for about 5 minutes, until it becomes transparent. Pour the sauce into the skillet using a strainer, then stir and season with the salt. Cook for 6 to 8 more minutes over very low heat. Set aside until you serve the chiles rellenos.

4. To make the peppers: Roast the poblano peppers over an open flame of your stove over medium-high heat, turning for even roasting, 8 to 10 minutes. Place the roasted peppers in a plastic bag and close it, letting them steam for 5 minutes. Remove from the bag and scrape off the charred skin by rubbing your fingers on the surface of the peppers. Using a sharp knife, cut a slit along the length of the peppers and remove the seeds and veins.

5. Stuff the peppers with the picadillo using a spoon. Do not overstuff them, or the filling can leak out of the pepper when frying it.

(continued)

6. Add the oil to a large skillet so that it is ¾ inch (2 cm) deep and heat over medium-high heat. While the oil heats up, beat the egg whites with a hand mixer in a large bowl until they form stiff peaks. Gently stir in the egg yolks, one by one, while beating. Continue beating until you have a fluffy batter.

7. Spread the flour on a large plate and lightly coat each pepper, shaking off any excess flour. Once all the peppers are coated with flour, dip them into the egg batter, making sure they are well coated.

8. Carefully place each pepper into the hot oil. Do not overcrowd the skillet. Fry each side of the peppers until the batter turns a deep golden color. This will take a few minutes per side. Use a large spatula to gently turn over the peppers. Once they are fried, place them on a paper towel–lined dish or tray to drain the oil.

9. To serve, spoon about 5 tablespoons (75 ml) of the tomato sauce on each plate and then place a chile relleno on top. Serve with the rice.

NOTAS

* *Do not buy large poblano peppers for this recipe, especially if this is your first time making them. They will not be easy to handle when frying, and they also lack flavor compared to the smaller ones. If you can, buy organic peppers; they taste the best.*

* *You can prepare the picadillo specially for these chiles rellenos or you can use leftover picadillo.*

* *Store any leftovers in a plastic or glass container in the refrigerator for up to 2 days. You can reheat them in a microwave for 2 minutes or in a conventional oven for 10 minutes at 350°F (175°C). You can reheat the sauce on the stove or in the microwave for 1 to 1½ minutes.*

MOLE POBLANO

Mole poblano is one of the most representative dishes of Mexico and its cuisine. The unique mixture of peppers, vegetables, spices, seeds, and chocolate make it a rich and exotic dish you need to try at least once in your lifetime. The preparation of mole poblano is generally a sign of a big celebration. I learned how to make it when I was very young from one of my aunts who lives in the state of Veracruz. You can use this mole for any recipe that calls for mole.

PREP TIME: 30 minutes	**COOK TIME:** 50 minutes	**YIELD:** 12 servings

CHICKEN

1 large roasting chicken (6 to 7 pounds/2.7 to 3.2 kg), cut into pieces

About 8 cups (2 quarts/1.9 L) water

1 small onion, cut into quarters

4 cloves garlic

1 sprig fresh cilantro

1 sprig fresh parsley

Salt, to taste

MOLE SAUCE

6 mulato peppers

4 ancho peppers

6 pasilla peppers

4 cups (1 quart/950 ml) chicken broth or water

1 tablet Mexican drinking chocolate (about 3.2 ounces/90 g)

¼ teaspoon coriander seeds

½ teaspoon anise seeds

¾ cup (100 g) sesame seeds

6 whole cloves

½ teaspoon black peppercorns

½ cup vegetable oil (120 ml) or lard (120 g), divided

½ cup (70 g) raisins

1. To make the chicken: Place all the chicken ingredients in a large stockpot over medium-high heat and bring to a boil. Reduce the heat to low, cover, and simmer until the chicken is just cooked through, about 35 minutes. Use a spoon to skim off any foam that forms on the surface. When the chicken is done, transfer it to a large bowl, cover, and set aside. Strain and reserve the broth in the pot; you will use it to make the mole sauce.

2. To make the mole sauce: It is important to have all the ingredients ready to go. Slice the peppers open using kitchen scissors or a knife, remove the seeds and the veins, and flatten them; this will help result in an even toasting. Reserve 1 tablespoon (5 g) of the seeds from the peppers to use for the sauce. Bring the reserved chicken broth to a simmer, to soak all the ingredients in. You will add the ingredients to the pot after toasting or frying them. The soaking will make them softer and easier to grind.

3. In a large skillet, toast the peppers a few at a time, on both sides, pressing them down as you turn them. They will quickly release their aroma. The toasting process takes only 30 to 40 seconds, so don't let the peppers burn. Place the toasted peppers and the chocolate in the pot with the broth to soak. Continue toasting the remainder of the peppers and placing them in the broth.

4. Separately toast the reserved pepper seeds, coriander seeds, anise seeds, sesame seeds, whole cloves, and peppercorns (each of these ingredients needs to be toasted separately). Reserve 2 tablespoons (16 g) of the toasted sesame seeds to use for garnishing. Place all the other toasted ingredients in the pot with the chicken broth.

(continued)

⅓ cup (45 g) whole unskinned almonds

⅓ cup (50 g) raw pumpkin seeds

⅓ cup (35 g) peanuts

1 Mexican cinnamon stick (1½ inches/ 4 cm long)

2 medium tomatoes

3 cloves garlic, unpeeled

½ medium white onion, sliced ¼ inch (6 mm) thick

1 corn tortilla

3 small slices bread (such as a French baguette or Mexican bolillo)

½ large ripe dark-skinned plantain, peeled and cut into thick slices

Salt, to taste

TO SERVE

Arroz Blanco (page 130) or Arroz Rojo (page 132), made with peas

Warm corn tortillas

NOTAS

* This mole sauce is not very spicy, so if you want to add some heat to the sauce, add 2 dried chipotle peppers or 2 morita peppers.

* Some recipes suggest frying the dried peppers instead of toasting them.

* If the mole gets too thick for your liking, add some chicken broth to make it thinner.

* Mole can be made the day before and refrigerated, and the leftover sauce can be kept in the freezer for about 4 months. When reheated, it will probably have to be diluted with some chicken broth.

5. Add 2 tablespoons of the oil (30 ml) or lard (30 g) to a large skillet and separately fry the raisins, almonds, pumpkin seeds, and peanuts; fry the raisins until they are plump, the almonds until they are well browned, the pumpkin seeds until they swell up (be careful, as they tend to explode and jump if heated too much), and the peanuts until they have a golden color. Drain any excess fat. Add these ingredients, along with the cinnamon stick, to the pot with the chicken broth.

6. Fry the tomatoes and roast the garlic cloves in the skillet for about 5 minutes. If you prefer, you can choose to either roast or fry both the ingredients. Peel the garlic and add it to the broth along with the fried tomato. Fry the onion until golden brown and place it in the pot. Fry the tortilla and the bread in whole pieces until crisp and golden brown. Only add a little more oil or lard at a time, or it will be absorbed by the tortilla and the bread. Add these to the pot. Add the plantain to the skillet and fry until golden, about 3 minutes. Drain, using a slotted spoon, and transfer it to the pot.

7. Once you have all the fried and toasted ingredients in the pot, you are ready to process them in a blender (it will look a bit messy). Add ½ cup (120 ml) of the chicken broth into the blender. Gradually add the mixture to the blender with a slotted spoon, and blend well, then add another ½ cup (120 ml) broth and continue to gradually blend the ingredients into a slightly fine paste. Try not to add any more liquid, unless your blender is having trouble blending the ingredients. Make sure to constantly free up the blades of the blender with a rubber spatula, in order to keep the blender from becoming stuck. You will have to do this in 2 or 3 batches until everything has been puréed. Blend the sauce one more time to get a smoother texture. If the end result is still coarse, pass the whole mixture through a strainer. You may not need to strain the sauce if you have a high-performance blender.

8. Add 2 tablespoons of the oil (30 ml) or lard (30 g) to a large pot or Dutch oven over medium heat. Add the mole sauce. Scrape the bottom of the pan often with a wooden spoon to keep the sauce from sticking. Taste and season with the salt. Stirring constantly, continue to cook the mole over low heat for 12 to 15 minutes, until it is very thick and becomes darker in color. The mixture will bubble and splutter, and pools of oil will form on the surface.

9. Add the cooked chicken to the hot mole and simmer until the chicken is heated through, about 10 minutes.

10. To serve, place a piece of chicken on a warm plate. Spoon on plenty of the mole sauce and sprinkle some of the reserved sesame seeds on top. Serve with the rice and tortillas.

ALBONDIGAS

Mexican Meatball Soup

There are several ways to make a Mexican meatball soup, and this is a simple recipe that my family absolutely loves. These meatballs are cooked in an aromatic tomato broth, flavored with fresh cilantro.

PREP TIME: 15 minutes	COOK TIME: 35 minutes	YIELD: 6 servings

BROTH

1 pound (450 g) tomatoes (about 3 medium tomatoes)

¼ medium white onion

1 clove garlic, unpeeled

¼ cup (60 ml) water, if needed

1 tablespoon (15 ml) vegetable oil

6 cups (1½ quarts/1.4 L) chicken broth

1 cup (115 g) large cubed carrot

1 cup (140 g) large cubed potato

1¼ cups (225 g) large cubed Mexican squash or zucchini

½ cup (20 g) chopped fresh cilantro

Salt, to taste

MEATBALLS

1 slice white sandwich bread

¼ cup (60 ml) whole milk

1 pound (450 g) ground beef

1 clove garlic, chopped (or ⅓ teaspoon garlic powder)

6 peppercorns (or ½ teaspoon ground pepper)

1 large egg, beaten

Salt, to taste

TO SERVE

Arroz Rojo (page 132) (optional)

Warm corn tortillas

1. To make the broth: Preheat a comal or large skillet over medium-high heat, then roast the tomatoes, onion, and garlic. (See page 16 for specific roasting instructions for each vegetable.) Peel the garlic and place the roasted vegetables in a blender. Blend until smooth. If your tomatoes aren't juicy enough and your blender is having a hard time blending, add the water.

2. Heat the oil in a large saucepan over medium-high heat. Add the sauce and cook for about 5 minutes, then add the chicken broth. When the broth starts to boil, reduce the heat to a simmer.

3. In the meantime, make the meatballs: In a small bowl, soak the bread with the milk until it is softened, about 1 minute. Place the ground beef into a large bowl and make a well in the center.

4. Pulverize the garlic clove and peppercorns in a molcajete (or use the ground spices). Add the ground spices to the well in the meat, along with the milk-soaked bread and beaten egg. Season with the salt. Gently mix the meat with the other ingredients using your hands or a wooden spoon. Do not overmix or your meatballs will be tough.

5. Form golf ball–size meatballs with your hands wetted with cold water, without forcing or putting too much pressure on the meat. As you form them, carefully drop them into the simmering tomato broth.

6. Add the carrots to the saucepan, and continue forming the meatballs, about 12 in total. Once all the meatballs are in the broth, add the potatoes. Continue cooking for 5 more minutes and stir in the squash, then simmer for another 10 to 12 minutes. About 5 minutes before everything is done cooking, add the chopped cilantro and season with the salt.

7. Serve in medium bowls, along with the rice (if using) or beans (if using) and warm corn tortillas.

NOTAS

✖ *I prefer to use ground beef that is 85% lean.*

✖ *You can add other diced vegetables, such as chayote and cabbage, to this soup while it's simmering in step 6.*

ALBONDIGAS EN CHIPOTLE

Meatballs in Chipotle Sauce

This is one of the most popular ways of eating meatballs in Mexico. The mild spiciness and smokiness of the chipotle peppers are the key flavors of this dish. If you like spicy food, you can always adjust the heat in this dish by adding more chipotle peppers.

PREP TIME: 20 minutes	**COOK TIME:** 25 minutes	**YIELD:** 6 servings

MEATBALLS

2 tablespoons (30 ml) whole milk

1 slice white sandwich bread

1 pound (450 g) ground beef

1 egg

Salt and pepper, to taste

1 clove garlic, minced, or ½ teaspoon garlic powder

CHIPOTLE SAUCE

3 large tomatoes, chopped

1 or 2 chipotle peppers in adobo sauce (from a can), depending on preferred spiciness

1½ tablespoons (22 ml) vegetable oil

¼ cup (30 g) finely chopped white onion

2 cloves garlic, minced

½ cup (120 ml) chicken broth or water, if needed

Salt and pepper, to taste.

GARNISHING AND TO SERVE

Chopped fresh parsley or cilantro

Arroz Rojo (page 132)

Green salad of choice

1. To make the meatballs: Place the milk and the bread in a large bowl, and mash the bread until smooth. Add the ground meat, along with the egg, salt, pepper, and garlic. Knead the ingredients with your hands until they are well combined.

2. Form 16 meatballs (about 1½ inch/4 cm in size) with your hands wetted with cold water.

3. To make the chipotle sauce: Place the tomatoes and chipotle peppers (no adobo sauce) in a blender, and blend until smooth.

4. Heat the oil in a large saucepan over medium-high heat. Add the onion and cook until transparent, about 5 minutes. Add the garlic, stir, and continue cooking for another 3 minutes. Stir in the chipotle sauce and simmer for 5 minutes. If your tomatoes aren't juicy enough and the sauce becomes dry, add about ⅓ cup (80 ml) chicken broth or water.

5. Add the meatballs to the saucepan, cover, and cook over low heat for 10 minutes. Season the sauce with the salt and pepper, then continue simmering, uncovered, for 10 more minutes. If the sauce is too thin, remove the already-cooked meatballs and keep simmering the sauce until the desired thickness is achieved. You can wrap the meatballs in aluminum foil and place them in a warm oven set at a low temperature while the sauce simmers.

6. Serve in medium bowls garnished with the parsley or cilantro, along with the rice and salad.

NOTAS

✖ *I prefer to use ground beef that is 85% lean.*

✖ *Many cooks like to stuff the meatballs with a small piece of hard-boiled egg or cheese, or even a small bit of serrano pepper. To do this, press the egg (or other filling) into the meatball when forming it in step 2, then seal it by rolling the meatball again between your hands.*

CALABACITAS CON PUERCO

Pork Stew with Squash

This is a beloved dish in many homes, and somehow the combination of pork with the vegetables makes for a simple yet memorable meal. In Mexico, *calabacitas* (squash) are used in many soups, stews, and other types of dishes. If you can't find Mexican squash, you can use zucchini, and it will still be delicious. In Spanish, this dish is sometimes called *calabacitas con puerco y elote*, because it also has corn in it. Some cooks do not add corn to the stew, and others will make it with a different salsa (it can be made with a red or green salsa).

PREP TIME: 10 minutes	**COOK TIME:** 55 minutes	**YIELD:** 6 servings

2 pounds (900 g) pork shoulder, cut into 1-inch (2.5 cm) cubes

1 cup (240 ml) water

1 bay leaf

2 tablespoons (30 ml) vegetable oil

1 cup (115 g) diced white or red onion (about ½ medium onion)

2 cloves garlic, minced

2 jalapeño peppers, diced

1 cup (140 g) fresh corn kernels (or canned corn, drained, or frozen corn, thawed)

2 medium Mexican squash or zucchini, cut into ½-inch (13 mm) cubes

1 pound (450 g) tomatoes, diced

1 sprig fresh cilantro

¼ teaspoon ground cumin

Salt and pepper, to taste

TO SERVE

Arroz Rojo (page 132)

Warm corn tortillas

1. Place the meat in a large skillet with the water and bay leaf. Cover and cook over medium heat for 20 minutes. If there's any liquid left over from cooking the meat, reserve it and set aside.

2. Add the oil to the pan and cook the meat over medium-high heat until it is slightly browned, stirring occasionally to keep it from sticking to the pan, 3 to 4 minutes.

3. Add the onion, garlic, and peppers to the pan. Cook for 3 minutes, stirring occasionally, until they have softened. Add the corn and cook for another 3 minutes. Add the squash and toss well. Continue cooking for 5 more minutes.

4. Stir in the tomatoes and the reserved cooking liquid, along with the cilantro and ground cumin. Reduce the heat to low, cover, and simmer until the pork and vegetables are tender, about 20 minutes. Season with the salt and pepper.

5. Serve on plates with the rice and tortillas.

NOTAS

✳ *You can substitute the pork with chicken thighs and drumsticks.*

✳ *If the pork renders some fat, you can use 2 tablespoons (30 g) in place of the vegetable oil in step 2.*

✳ *Some cooks like to season this stew with Mexican oregano instead of cilantro, while others prefer epazote or Mexican mint.*

CARNE CON PAPAS

Beef and Potatoes

Considered a comfort food by many, *carne con papas* is a delicious mixture of meat and potatoes, simmered in a rich tomato sauce. This is another recipe that reminds me of my mother. When we were growing up, she had to find ways to feed her large family while on a tight budget, so she incorporated potatoes in many of her dishes, including stews like this one. Carne con papas is an excellent example of a hearty meal made with simple and affordable ingredients.

PREP TIME: 15 minutes	**COOK TIME:** 45 minutes	**YIELD:** 6 servings

1½ pounds (675 g) beef chuck roast, trimmed and cut into 1½-inch (4 cm) cubes

Salt and pepper, to taste

2 tablespoons (30 ml) vegetable oil

4 large tomatoes, chopped

½ cup (60 g) chopped white onion

2 cloves garlic

1 cup (240 ml) chicken broth, plus more if needed

2 large potatoes, cut into 1-inch (2.5 cm) cubes

2 serrano peppers

½ cup (20 g) chopped fresh cilantro

TO SERVE

Arroz Rojo (page 132) or Arroz Blanco (page 130)

Warm corn tortillas

1. Season the beef with the salt and pepper. Heat the oil in a large skillet or casserole over medium-high heat. Add the meat cubes to the pan and cook until they're browned on all sides, about 10 minutes.

2. While the meat is cooking, place the tomatoes, onion, garlic, and chicken broth in a blender. Blend until smooth.

3. Pour this sauce into the pan with the meat using a strainer. Bring the sauce to a simmer and cook, covered, for about 20 minutes. Add more broth if the sauce is too thick.

4. Stir in the potatoes and peppers, and continue cooking until the meat and potatoes are tender, about 15 minutes, continually stirring throughout the cooking process. Just before serving, stir in the cilantro and season with salt and pepper.

5. Serve on plates with the rice and tortillas.

NOTAS

✱ *Instead of adding the serrano peppers to the stew with the potatoes in step 4, the peppers can be blended into the sauce in step 2 if you want the dish to be a little spicy.*

✱ *In place of the cilantro, you can use herbs like oregano, bay leaf, or thyme.*

ASADO DE PUERCO

Pork Stew

This is a popular stew made with chunks of pork that are cooked until tender in a rich, dark sauce made with dried peppers and several spices. It is common in the northern states of Mexico, particularly in rural areas, where it is sometimes made for birthdays and weddings (it's also known as *asado de boda*, meaning "wedding stew"). I still remember the first time I tried this dish at the home of one of my aunts, where she served it in flour tortilla tacos and topped them with Salsa Verde (page 125).

PREP TIME: 20 minutes	**COOK TIME:** 1 hour 10 minutes	**YIELD:** 6 servings

2 pounds (900 g) boneless pork shoulder, cut into 1½-inch (4 cm) cubes

2 tablespoons vegetable oil (30 ml) or lard (30 g)

4 ancho peppers

4 guajillo peppers

1¼ cups (300 ml) water, divided, plus more as needed

3 cloves garlic

8 peppercorns

1 teaspoon dried Mexican oregano

2 cloves

2 bay leaves

½ teaspoon cumin seeds

½ inch (13 mm) cinnamon stick

½ teaspoon dried thyme

2 tablespoons (30 ml) vinegar

⅛ avocado pit (optional)

Salt, to taste

TO SERVE

Arroz Rojo (page 132)

Frijoles de la Olla (made with pinto beans) (page 138)

Warm corn tortillas (optional)

1. Place the pork pieces in a large stockpot and add enough water to cover the meat. Cook over medium-high heat until the meat is tender and the water has evaporated, 45 to 50 minutes. If the meat still isn't soft and tender, add more water and continue cooking. Once the pork is done, add the oil and continue cooking over medium heat until the meat is slightly browned.

2. While the pork is cooking, preheat a comal or large skillet over medium-high heat. Slice open the ancho and guajillo peppers and remove the seeds and veins. Slightly roast the peppers open wide in the pan for 30 to 40 seconds, then remove promptly. Place the peppers in a bowl and fill with enough hot water to cover them. Let soak for about 20 minutes. Drain thoroughly.

3. Add ¾ cup (180 ml) of the water to a blender, then add half of the peppers, along with the garlic, peppercorns, oregano, cloves, bay leaves, cumin, cinnamon stick, thyme, vinegar, and piece of avocado pit (if using). Blend for at least 1 minute, until smooth. Add the remaining ½ cup (120 ml) water and blend for a few more seconds to mix thoroughly. Add the remaining peppers, a little at a time, and continue blending until smooth, adding more water as needed to mix thoroughly.

4. Pass the sauce through a strainer, then add it to the pot with the browned meat. Cook over medium heat for 10 minutes, stirring frequently to prevent it from sticking to the pot. Add more water as needed and season with the salt. Keep stirring until the sauce thickens to the consistency of a thick gravy, about 15 minutes.

5. Serve on plates with the rice and beans, with the tortillas (if using) on the side.

NOTAS

✖ *The avocado pit adds a little thickness to the sauce, as well as a bit of a tart flavor.*

✖ *Some cooks like to add a little piece of orange peel to the stew for more flavor.*

✖ *If you have a high-performance blender, you can process the sauce in step 3 all at once, pouring 2 cups (480 ml) water into the blender along with the peppers and spices.*

MILANESA DE RES

Beef Milanesa

Milanesas are a kid's favorite meal, even more so if you serve them with a side of fried potatoes or spaghetti. A universal comfort food, this is a meal that you will almost always find served at local diners and small eateries called *cocinas economicas*, where people have their main meals during the midafternoon. They will usually offer beef or chicken varieties. This recipe is the way my mother made breaded beef steaks, using a seasoning of freshly ground garlic and peppercorns. She also preferred using saltine crackers for the breading.

PREP TIME: 15 minutes	**COOK TIME:** 20 minutes	**YIELD:** 6 servings

2 cloves garlic, chopped

½ teaspoon black peppercorns

1 tablespoon (15 ml) water

2 eggs

2 cups (230 g) dried bread crumbs or crushed saltines

Salt, to taste

1½ pounds (675 g) thinly cut top round beef steaks (6 steaks)

Vegetable oil, for frying

TO SERVE

Fried potatoes of your choice

Green salad of your choice

1. Grind the garlic and peppercorns in a molcajete or finely chop the garlic and use a pepper grinder for the black peppercorns (or you can use ½ teaspoon ground pepper). Add the water to the ground ingredients to form a paste.

2. In a large bowl, lightly whisk the eggs, then add the garlic and pepper mixture. Whisk again.

3. In a large dish, spread out the bread crumbs mixed with the salt (use salt only if using regular bread crumbs; do not add if using saltines) and have another dish ready to place the steaks on after breading (I use wax paper to cover the second plate for an easy clean-up afterward).

4. For the breading process, dip a steak into the egg and pepper mixture. Using kitchen tongs, dredge the steak in the bread crumbs, then turn over to coat both sides. Lightly pat the steak when breading to make sure that the coating adheres to the steak. If necessary, turn the steak over again for an even coating. Place the breaded steak on the prepared plate. Repeat this process with the remaining steaks.

5. Heat ½ inch (13 mm) of oil in a large skillet over medium-high heat. Make sure the oil is hot before adding the steaks. Fry the steaks for about 3 minutes per side, until they are cooked through and golden brown all over. Place the steaks on a paper towel–lined plate to drain the excess oil.

6. Serve the steaks with the warm fried potatoes and salad.

NOTAS

✖ You can also use sirloin steaks, chicken, and pork to make the milanesas; just make sure to pound them very thin.

✖ In Mexico, milanesas are usually sold in some butcher shops or supermarkets already breaded for frying. You can also find them in the United States in the meat section of some Latin stores.

✖ I usually freeze already-breaded milanesas (uncooked) for later. They will keep up to 6 weeks and need to be thawed before frying.

CAMARONES EN CHIPOTLE

Shrimp in Chipotle Sauce

This dish, also called "deviled shrimp," can be made with other types of peppers, like puya or árbol. Because this recipe uses shrimp, it is best to have all your ingredients prepped before adding the shrimp, as they tend to cook quickly.

PREP TIME: 15 minutes	COOK TIME: 25 minutes	YIELD: 4 servings

1 pound (450 g) raw shrimp (about 16 large shrimp), cleaned and deveined

1 tablespoon (15 ml) fresh lime juice

Salt and pepper, to taste

2 medium tomatoes

1 clove garlic

2 chipotle peppers in adobo sauce (from a can)

2 tablespoons (30 ml) olive oil, divided

⅓ cup (40 g) finely chopped white onion

¼ teaspoon dried thyme

GARNISHING AND TO SERVE

Arroz Blanco (page 130)

Chopped fresh parsley or cilantro

1. In a large bowl, combine the shrimp with the lime juice and season with the salt and pepper. Let rest for 15 minutes to marinate.

2. Preheat a comal or large skillet over medium-high heat. Roast the tomatoes in the pan, turning them every 2 minutes or so, to allow for even roasting, for a total of 8 minutes. Combine the roasted tomatoes, garlic, and chipotle peppers in a blender, along with some of the adobo sauce from the peppers. Blend until smooth, then set aside.

3. Heat 1 tablespoon (15 ml) of the oil in a large skillet over medium-high heat. Add the onion and shrimp (without the marinated juices). Slightly cook the shrimp, turning quickly to avoid overcooking, about 4 minutes (the shrimp will continue to cook in step 5). Transfer the shrimp to a plate and set aside.

4. Add the remaining 1 tablespoon (15 ml) oil to the skillet. Add the tomato sauce, stirring constantly to prevent it from sticking to the bottom of the pan. Simmer for about 10 minutes.

5. Add the thyme and season with salt, then add the shrimp and cook for 2 more minutes (do not overcook the shrimp or they will have a rubbery texture).

6. Serve over the white rice and sprinkle with the chopped parsley or cilantro.

NOTA *You can add ¼ cup (60 ml) white wine to the sauce, then let the sauce reduce a little bit longer. If you choose to do this, add the wine when you add the thyme and salt in step 5, just before adding the shrimp to the sauce.*

BISTEC A LA MEXICANA

Mexican-Style Steak

Bistec a la Mexicana is an easy meal to prepare. It consists of beef tips cooked in a rich sauce made with tomatoes, onion, garlic, and serrano peppers that pairs divinely with the tender meat. Dishes are called *a la Mexicana* when they use a combination of tomatoes, peppers, and onions, because their colors represent those of the Mexican flag (green, white, and red). This recipe only requires a few ingredients and a short amount of time to make. This dish, along with Picadillo (page 99), is one of my favorite go-to meals when I'm in a hurry.

PREP TIME: 15 minutes plus 1 hour marinating time	**COOK TIME:** 25 minutes	**YIELD:** 6 servings

½ teaspoon black peppercorns

¼ teaspoon cumin seeds (optional)

2 cloves garlic

2 pounds (900 g) beef tenderloin tips

Salt, to taste

2 tablespoons (30 ml) vegetable or olive oil

½ medium white onion, chopped

4 serrano peppers, chopped

4 large tomatoes, chopped

TO SERVE

Arroz Rojo (page 132)

Frijoles Pintos Cremosos (page 140)

Warm corn or flour tortillas (optional)

Warm crusty bread (French baguette or crusty Mexican bolillos) (optional)

1. Using a molcajete, grind the black peppercorns with the cumin (if using). Add the garlic, crush it, and keep grinding to form a paste with the spices.

2. Add the paste to the beef tips in a large bowl and mix together. Add the salt and let marinate for at least 1 hour in the refrigerator (if you're short on time, 10 to 15 minutes will do).

3. Heat the oil in a large skillet over medium-high heat. Add the onion and cook for about 3 minutes, then add the marinated beef tips. Cook until the beef is browned, about 8 minutes.

4. Add the serrano peppers and cook for 2 more minutes, then add the tomatoes and season with salt. Cook for about 12 more minutes, until the sauce thickens and the meat is tender.

5. Serve this dish with the rice, beans, and tortillas (if using) or crusty bread (if using).

NOTAS

✱ *You can also use other cuts of beef for this stew, such as rib eye, sirloin, and beef chuck. The cooking times will vary because each cut has a different texture.*

✱ *You may be tempted to use garlic powder and ground black pepper instead of the fresh versions, but I assure you that using the fresh ingredients will render an incredibly tastier dish.*

CHICHARRÓN EN SALSA VERDE

Fried Pork Skins in Green Salsa

This is a hugely popular dish in Mexico. It's great by itself, but it is also used as a filling for gorditas, tacos, and sometimes even tortas. You can find it in pretty much any city, at a variety of restaurants, diners, and markets. In my home, we like to enjoy this dish served in a bowl with pinto beans. This is how my husband and I used to order it at an old eatery when we were living in Toluca, near Mexico City.

PREP TIME: 15 minutes	**COOK TIME:** 30 minutes	**YIELD:** 4 servings

12 ounces (340 g) tomatillos (about 8 medium tomatillos), husks removed

2 serrano peppers or 1 jalapeño pepper

1 clove garlic

⅛ whole plus ¼ finely chopped medium white onion, divided

4 cups (1 quart/950 ml) water, divided

1 tablespoon (15 ml) vegetable oil

2 cups (30 g) chicharrones, broken into small pieces

Salt, to taste

TO SERVE

Warm corn tortillas

Cooked pinto beans

1. Place the tomatillos, peppers, garlic, and ⅛ onion in a large saucepan. Cover with 4 cups (950 ml) of the water, turn the heat to high, and bring to a boil. Reduce the heat and gently simmer for about 15 minutes, until the tomatillos are cooked.

2. Allow the ingredients in the saucepan to cool, then transfer them to a blender with 2 cups (480 ml) of the cooking water and blend until smooth. Do not add more water.

3. Heat the oil in a large skillet over medium-high heat. Add the remaining ¼ chopped onion and cook, without browning, until soft, about 2 minutes. Add the sauce and cook over high heat, stirring from time to time, until the sauce is reduced and thickened, about 6 minutes.

4. Stir in the chicharrones and season with the salt. Continue cooking over medium heat until the chicharrones are softer. This will take 10 to 12 minutes, depending on the thickness and freshness of the chicharrón. The fat from the pork crackling will float to the surface of the sauce. If you prefer the sauce to be thinner, add more water, about ½ cup (120 ml), while cooking.

5. Serve with the tortillas and beans.

NOTA *Store any leftovers in the refrigerator for up to 2 days.*

DISCADA NORTEÑA

Northern-Style Mixed Meats

In the northern states of Mexico, people love grilling their meats. During the time I lived there, there was not a single weekend when you couldn't open the door without smelling the aroma of burning mesquite charcoal. The grilling would begin on Friday afternoon and last the whole weekend. This dish is made with several grilled meats in a rich tomato-based sauce. It is called *discada* because it was originally made using a metal plowing disc. The hole in the center would be welded shut, and after the disc was seasoned, it could then be used for cooking, similar to a wok. These days, you can find disc cooking pans sold in many stores and markets throughout Mexico, as well as in some parts of the United States.

PREP TIME: 15 minutes	**COOK TIME:** 40 minutes	**YIELD:** 6 servings

2 tablespoons vegetable oil (30 ml) or lard (30 g)

2 thick bacon slices, diced

1 chorizo link (about 2 ounces/55 g), crumbled

8 ounces (225 g) pork shoulder, cut into small cubes

1 pound (450 g) sirloin or rib-eye steak, cut into small cubes

1 cup (115 g) diced white onion

1 green bell pepper, seeded, veins removed, and diced

2 serrano peppers, diced

2 hot dogs, cut into bite-size pieces

2 pounds (900 g) chopped fresh tomatoes

1 cup (240 ml) light-colored beer of your choice, at room temperature

Salt and pepper, to taste

⅓ cup (13 g) chopped fresh cilantro

1. Heat the oil in a large skillet over medium-high heat. Add the bacon and cook until crispy. Remove the bacon from the pan and place it on a paper towel–lined plate to drain the excess fat.

2. In the same skillet, cook the chorizo for 5 to 6 minutes. Remove it from the pan and place it on the same plate as the bacon.

3. Add the pork to the skillet and cook for about 7 minutes, then remove from the pan and place on a separate plate from the other cooked meats. Don't worry if it doesn't look done yet; it will finish cooking with the rest of the ingredients later.

4. Add the beef to the skillet and cook for 8 minutes. Remove and place with the cooked meats.

5. Add the onion and peppers to the skillet and cook for about 3 minutes. Add the cooked meat, hot dogs, and the tomatoes. Cook for about 10 more minutes (by this time, the tomatoes will start releasing their juices).

6. Pour in the beer, season with the salt and pepper, and cover. Continue cooking for another 5 minutes until all the meats are tender and well cooked. Just before serving, stir in the chopped cilantro.

7. Serve in medium bowls, alongside the guacamole, beans, and tortillas.

TO SERVE

Guacamole (page 129) or sliced
avocado (optional)

Beans of your choice

Warm flour tortillas

Guacamole (page 129)

NOTAS

✖ *I usually make this dish on my kitchen stove, but if you can make it over a charcoal grill, the flavors will taste even better.*

✖ *This recipe is a great way to reuse any leftover meats you have from your weekend barbecuing, which will add that extra smoky flavor to this dish.*

✖ *In addition to hot dogs, you can also add other types of sausages, including smoked ones.*

ENTOMATADAS

This is another recipe from my mom, a woman who always offered something to eat to visitors. *Entomatadas* was one of her favorite dishes to make for her kids, since they're so easy to make. The process is similar to making enchiladas. Entomatadas are corn tortillas that are folded (or rolled), stuffed with cheese, and covered in a tomato sauce.

PREP TIME: 10 minutes	**COOK TIME:** 30 minutes	**YIELD:** 6 servings

1½ pounds (675 g) tomatoes

1 serrano pepper

2 small cloves garlic

¾ cup (90 g) finely chopped white onion, divided

8 ounces (225 g) queso fresco or farmer cheese, crumbled

4 tablespoons (60 ml) vegetable oil, divided

Salt, to taste

12 corn tortillas

NOTAS

✖ *I add a serrano pepper to the sauce because this is the way my mom made it. You can skip the pepper if you like.*

✖ *You can warm the tortillas in a skillet instead of frying them. This is how my mom does it.*

1. Place the tomatoes, pepper, and garlic in a saucepan and cover with water. Cook over medium heat for 15 to 20 minutes, until the ingredients are soft.

2. In a medium bowl, combine ¼ cup (30 g) of the onion with the crumbled cheese and set aside.

3. Place the cooked tomatoes, pepper, and garlic in a blender, and blend until a smooth. Set aside.

4. Heat 1 tablespoon (15 ml) of the oil in a large skillet over medium-high heat. Add the remaining ½ cup (60 g) onion and cook until transparent and slightly browned, about 5 minutes.

5. Add the tomato sauce to the skillet and cook for about 2 more minutes. Season with the salt, then reduce the heat to low and simmer for 6 to 8 minutes.

6. In a separate large skillet, heat the remaining 3 tablespoons (45 ml) oil over medium heat and briefly fry the tortillas, one by one, about 30 seconds each, and place them on a paper towel–lined plate to drain the excess oil.

7. Dip a fried tortilla into the warm tomato sauce in the other skillet. Flip over the tortilla to cover both sides with the tomato sauce. Place the tortilla on a large plate and spoon some of the onion and cheese mixture onto it. Fold the tortilla in half to form the entomatada. Repeat this process with the remaining tortillas and filling.

8. To serve, spoon some of the leftover sauce over the entomatadas and top with more of the onion and cheese mixture.

EMPANADAS DE QUESO

Cheese Empanadas

These simplest of empanadas are made using a recipe from the state of Tabasco, on Mexico's Gulf Coast. They are a perfect meatless treat for parties or large dinners. One thing about this recipe that some people might find peculiar is the addition of sugar to the cheese filling. It may sound weird at first, but the balance between the sweetness of the sugar and the saltiness of the cheese and corn dough makes for a delicious bite.

PREP TIME: 20 minutes	**COOK TIME:** 20 minutes	**YIELD:** 12 empanadas

1½ cups (185 g) masa harina

1¼ cups (300 ml) warm water, plus more if needed (see Notas)

¼ teaspoon salt

½ cup (120 ml) vegetable oil, for cooking the empanadas

2 cups (225 g) cold crumbled queso fresco

4 teaspoons sugar

GARNISHING AND TO SERVE

2 cups (120 g) shredded green cabbage or lettuce

1 tablespoon (15 ml) fresh lime juice

¼ medium onion, sliced

1 plum tomato, sliced

Spicy salsa of your choice

¼ cup (30 g) crumbled Cotija cheese or queso fresco

1. Mix together the masa harina, warm water, and salt in a large bowl. Knead well until the dough is smooth and soft. Divide the dough into 12 equal-size balls and cover them with a damp cloth towel.

2. Heat the oil in a large skillet over medium-high heat.

3. To make the filling for the empanadas, combine the queso fresco with the sugar in a medium bowl.

4. To form the empanadas, place a ball of masa harina between two plastic sheets cut from a freezer bag (see photo on page 18) in a tortilla press. Press down on the tortilla press to form a circle, then remove the top plastic sheet. Place 2 tablespoons (15 g) of the cheese and sugar mixture in the center of the circle. With the help of the bottom plastic sheet, fold the circle in half and seal the edges well. (It is important to seal the edges well, because if the filling leaks out when frying, it can cause the oil to splatter.) Repeat this process with the remaining dough balls and filling, while frying the formed empanadas.

5. Lower an empanada into the hot oil and cook until the bottom is golden brown, then turn it over to cook the other side, about 2 minutes per side (you can fry more than one at a time; just don't overcrowd the pan). Remove from the pan and place on a paper towel–lined plate to drain the excess oil. Continue frying the rest of the empanadas.

6. Right before serving, mix the shredded cabbage with the lime juice in a bowl. Serve the empanadas topped with the cabbage, the sliced onion and tomato, a drizzle of salsa, and a sprinkle of cheese.

NOTAS

* *Make sure that the queso fresco for the filling is cold. This will keep it from melting too easily and oozing out of the empanadas when frying them.*

* *You may need to add a couple more tablespoons (30 ml) of water as you knead the dough for it to have a nice, soft texture. The amount needed will depend on whether you live in a humid or dry environment.*

* *Empanadas can be refrigerated for up to 3 days and frozen for up to 6 weeks. To reheat, completely defrost and heat on a comal or in a skillet, turning once, until warmed, about 10 minutes. They can also be reheated in an oven at 350°F (175°C) for 15 minutes.*

EMPANADAS DE CARNE MOLIDA

Ground Beef Empanadas

You can eat corn empanadas at any time of the day, but most Mexicans prefer to eat them at breakfast or dinner time. The varieties of fillings for corn dough empanadas are endless and include the classic cheese filling, shredded chicken, ground beef or pork, mushrooms, squash blossoms, Picadillo (page 99), and even fish and shrimp. You can also create your own unique empanadas using leftovers from last night's dinner.

PREP TIME: 30 minutes	**COOK TIME:** 30 minutes	**YIELD:** 12 empanadas

FILLING

1 pound (450 g) ground beef

Salt and pepper, to taste

1 tablespoon (15 ml) vegetable oil

¼ cup (30 g) finely chopped white onion

2 small cloves garlic, minced

¾ cup (125 g) diced tomato

2 tablespoons (6 g) chopped fresh cilantro

DOUGH

1½ cups (150 g) masa harina

1¼ cups (300 ml) warm water, plus more if needed (see Notas)

¼ teaspoon salt

½ cup (120 ml) vegetable oil, for frying the empanadas

GARNISHING AND TO SERVE

2 cups (120 g) shredded green cabbage or lettuce

¼ medium onion, sliced

1 plum tomato, sliced

Spicy salsa of your choice

1. To make the filling: Season the ground beef with the salt and pepper. Heat the oil in a large skillet over medium-high heat, then add the chopped onion and cook for 2 minutes. Stir in the garlic and cook for 1 more minute. Add the ground beef to the pan and increase the heat to high. Cook for 5 more minutes, stirring often to break up any bigger pieces of meat.

2. Add the diced tomato and continue cooking for 2 minutes. Once everything comes to a boil, reduce the heat to medium-low, check the seasoning, and add more salt and pepper if needed. Cover the skillet and gently simmer for 10 minutes, until all the juices from the meat and tomatoes have reduced. Stir in the chopped cilantro, remove from the heat, and set aside to cool before forming the empanadas.

3. To make the dough: Mix together the masa harina, warm water, and salt in a large bowl. Knead well until the dough is smooth and soft. Divide the dough into 12 equal-size balls and cover them with a damp cloth towel.

4. Heat the oil in a large skillet over medium-high heat.

5. To form the empanadas, place a ball of dough between two plastic sheets cut from a freezer bag (see photo on page 18) in a tortilla press. Press down on the tortilla press to form a circle, then remove the top plastic sheet. Place 2 tablespoons (18 g) of the ground beef in the center of the dough circle. With the help of the bottom plastic sheet, fold the circle in half and seal the edges well. (It is important to seal the edges well, because if the filling leaks out when frying, it can cause the oil to splatter.) Repeat this process with the remaining dough balls and filling, while frying the formed empanadas.

NOTAS

* *You may need to add a couple more tablespoons (30 ml) of water as you knead the dough for it to have a nice, soft texture. The amount needed will depend on whether you live in a humid or dry environment.*

* *See Notas on page 81 for storage and reheating instructions.*

6. Lower an empanada into the hot oil and cook until the bottom is golden brown, then turn it over to cook the other side, about 2 minutes per side (you can fry more than one at a time; just don't overcrowd the pan). Remove from the pan and place on a paper towel–lined plate to drain the excess oil. Continue frying the rest of the empanadas.

7. Serve the empanadas while they are warm. Top them with the cabbage, onion, and tomato, and accompany with the salsa.

TOSTADAS DE POLLO

Chicken Tostadas

For many people, comfort food is a warm bowl of chicken soup or a hearty stew with mashed potatoes. For me, it's tostadas; they're my all-time favorite comfort food. The crunchiness of the tostada, the creaminess of the beans, the freshness of the lettuce: there's just something about the combination of all those textures and flavors in this dish that I can't resist. Tostadas are also easy to make, and there is a wide variety of toppings to choose from. You can top your tostada with shredded beef, ground beef, pork, shrimp, mushrooms, tuna, or just creamy refried beans.

PREP TIME: 20 minutes	**YIELD:** 12 tostadas (4 servings)

1 pound (450 g) boneless, skinless chicken breasts, cooked and shredded

Salt and pepper, to taste

¼ teaspoon garlic powder (optional)

¼ teaspoon onion powder (optional)

1 cup (240 g) refried beans (black or pinto), warmed

12 corn tostadas

2 cups (85 g) shredded lettuce

1 large tomato, sliced or diced

1 avocado, peeled, pitted, and sliced (cut just before serving time)

½ cup (60 g) crumbled queso fresco

GARNISHING AND TO SERVE

Mexican crema

Salsa of your choice

Pickled jalapeños and carrots

1. Season the shredded chicken breast with the salt and pepper, as well as the garlic and onion powders (if using).

2. Spread about a tablespoon (15 g) of refried beans on each of the tostadas.

3. Top the tostadas with the shredded chicken, lettuce, a tomato slice, avocado slice, and crumbled cheese.

4. Just before serving, drizzle the tostadas with the Mexican crema. Serve them with the salsa and pickled jalapeños and carrots.

NOTAS

* *To save time, use store-bought rotisserie chicken breast to make this dish.*
* *The use of garlic powder and onion powder is optional, but they make the chicken extra flavorful.*

ENCHILADAS ROJAS

Red Enchiladas

This is one of those dishes that is cooked differently in every home. Each cook has their own recipe, and this is my version based on my mom's way of cooking them. In my hometown of Tampico, it is typical to have enchiladas for breakfast or brunch.

PREP TIME: 15 minutes	**COOK TIME:** 20 minutes	**YIELD:** 4 servings

4 guajillo peppers, sliced open, seeded, and veins removed

4 ancho peppers, sliced open, seeded, and veins removed

2 cloves garlic, chopped

½ cup (120 ml) water

¼ teaspoon dried Mexican oregano

Salt and pepper, to taste

About 5 tablespoons (75 ml) vegetable oil, divided

12 corn tortillas

1½ cups (180 g) crumbled queso fresco

GARNISHING AND TO SERVE

¼ cup (30 g) crumbled queso fresco

¼ cup (30 g) finely chopped white onion

1 cup (60 g) finely shredded lettuce or green cabbage (optional)

4 radishes, thinly sliced (optional)

Fried carrots and potatoes (see Notas) (optional)

1. Preheat a comal or large skillet over medium-high heat, then place the guajillo and ancho peppers open wide in the pan and slightly roast them for 30 to 40 seconds. Remove promptly. Place the peppers in a medium saucepan and cover with water, turn the heat to medium, and simmer for about 15 minutes, or until they look soft. Remove the saucepan from the heat and let the peppers cool in the water in the pan for another 10 to 15 minutes.

2. Drain the peppers and place them in a blender with the garlic. Add the ½ cup (120 ml) water (not from the saucepan) and blend until smooth. Pour the sauce into a large bowl using a strainer. Season with the oregano, salt, and pepper. Set aside.

3. Heat 2 tablespoons (30 ml) of the vegetable oil in a large skillet over medium heat. To fry the tortillas, it is better to add the oil little by little as needed; too much oil will result in soggy tortillas.

4. Dip the tortillas, one by one, into the bowl of enchilada sauce to lightly coat each side. Using kitchen tongs, place a tortilla in the skillet to briefly fry it for a few seconds on both sides. Add more vegetable oil to the skillet as needed. Place the fried tortilla on a large paper towel–lined plate to drain the excess oil. Repeat this step with the remaining tortillas.

5. To assemble the enchiladas, place 2 tablespoons (15 g) of cheese close to one edge of the tortilla and then roll it. Repeat this process with the remaining tortillas and filling. Arrange the enchiladas in a serving dish.

6. Mix together the queso fresco and finely chopped onion to use as a garnish. Sprinkle this mixture on top of the enchiladas and garnish them with the lettuce (if using) and radishes (if using). Serve with the fried carrots and potatoes.

NOTAS

* You can play around with the sauce until you find the taste that you and your family enjoy the most. You can use more ancho peppers than guajillo peppers, or the other way around, or even only one type of pepper.

* The sauce can be made 2 days in advance and refrigerated. It also freezes well for up to 2 months.

* Crumbled cheese is the traditional filling, but you can use other fillings, like shredded beef, chicken, or pork. If you want to add shredded meat, use 2 cups (300 g).

* To make the fried potatoes and carrots to serve with the enchiladas, start with 2 cups (280 g) peeled and cubed potatoes and 2 cups (230 g) peeled and cubed carrots. Boil them in a saucepan until almost tender, but still firm, then drain and cool. Using the same skillet you fried the enchiladas in, add a little more oil. Lightly fry the potatoes and carrots for 5 minutes. They will be coated in some of the sauce that remained in the skillet, giving them a unique and tasty flavor. Season with salt and garnish with Cotija cheese.

ENCHILADAS VERDES

Green Enchiladas

These enchiladas are filled with chicken, bathed in a creamy salsa verde and covered with cheese, before being baked in the oven. The melted Swiss cheese on top is what sets these enchiladas apart from others, which are usually garnished with crumbled cheeses. A beautiful and decadent dish, these *enchiladas verdes* are also known in Mexico by the name *enchiladas Suizas*, meaning Swiss enchiladas.

PREP TIME: 15 minutes	**COOK TIME:** 45 minutes	**YIELD:** 4 servings

12 ounces (340 g) tomatillos (about 8 medium tomatillos), husks removed

2 serrano peppers or 1 jalapeño pepper

1 clove garlic

⅛ medium white onion

4 cups (1 quart/950 ml) water

½ cup (120 ml) Mexican crema or sour cream

½ cup (20 g) chopped fresh cilantro

2 tablespoons (30 ml) vegetable oil, for frying

12 corn tortillas

2 cups (300 g) cooked and shredded chicken

Salt and pepper, to taste

¼ teaspoon onion powder

¼ teaspoon garlic powder

1 cup (115 g) shredded Swiss cheese

GARNISHING AND TO SERVE

½ medium red onion, thinly sliced

Chopped fresh cilantro

1. Place the tomatillos, peppers, garlic, onion, and water in a large saucepan over high heat. Bring to a boil, then reduce the heat and gently simmer for about 15 minutes, until the tomatillos are cooked. Allow the ingredients to cool, then remove them from the saucepan using a slotted spoon and place them in the blender, along with 1 cup (240 ml) of the cooking water. Blend until smooth. Add the Mexican crema and the cilantro to the blender, and blend again until all ingredients are a uniform texture. Set aside.

2. Heat the oil in a large skillet over medium heat. Using a pair of kitchen tongs, dip the tortillas, one at a time, into the oil to soften them. They only need to be in the oil for a few seconds per side (aside from softening them for easy rolling, this prevents the tortillas from breaking apart). Transfer the tortillas to a plate lined with paper towels to drain the excess oil. Preheat the oven to 350°F (175°C).

3. Season the chicken with the salt, pepper, and onion and garlic powders. Spread about a third of the sauce in the bottom of a 9 x 11-inch (23 x 28 cm) baking dish.

4. To assemble the enchiladas, place some chicken on a tortilla, close to one edge, and roll it up to form an enchilada. Place the enchilada, seam side down, in the baking dish. Repeat this process with the remaining tortillas and chicken, until the baking dish is filled with a layer of the rolled enchiladas. Cover the enchiladas with the rest of the sauce, then sprinkle on the cheese. Bake in the oven for 30 minutes, or until the cheese starts to turn golden brown.

5. Garnish with the sliced onion and the cilantro, and serve immediately.

NOTAS

* Some people like to add a roasted poblano pepper to the sauce.

* To save time, use store-bought rotisserie chicken to make this dish.

* Instead of passing the tortillas through the oil, you can brush them with oil, then warm them in a skillet. This method uses less oil.

* Instead of Swiss cheese, you can use Muenster or Monterey Jack, or any combination of these. You can also use sliced cheese instead of shredded cheese.

* Serve the enchiladas with Mexican crema or sour cream, drizzling it over the enchiladas to cool down the spiciness of the salsa.

* The enchiladas can be prepared ahead of time, covered tightly, and stored in the refrigerator for 2 days until you're ready to bake them in step 4. Just make sure that you use a good-quality tortilla that won't break apart in the sauce.

COSTILLAS EN SALSA VERDE

Pork Rib Tips in Green Salsa

Pork rib tips is a popular cut of meat in Mexico, because of its affordability and rich flavor. This stew made with salsa verde is a staple in many homes, and that means that there are as many variations to this recipe as there are home cooks in Mexico. You can switch out the vegetables in this recipe to make it your own; instead of the nopales, substitute squash, zucchini, green beans, or chayotes.

PREP TIME: 10 minutes	**COOK TIME:** 50 minutes	**YIELD:** 6 servings

2 pounds (900 g) pork rib tips

2 cups (480 ml) water

3 cloves garlic (1 peeled and 2 unpeeled), divided

1 bay leaf

¼ plus ⅓ medium white onion, divided

2 tablespoons vegetable oil (30 ml) or rendered pork fat (30 g)

1 pound (450 g) tomatillos (about 11 medium tomatillos), husks removed

4 to 6 serrano or 2 to 3 jalapeño peppers

⅓ cup (13 g) chopped fresh cilantro

Salt and pepper, to taste

1½ cups (225 g) diced and cooked nopales (see page 9 for nopales prep)

TO SERVE

Arroz Blanco (page 130)

Warm corn tortillas

1. Chop the rib tips into 1½ inch (4 cm) sections and place them in a large saucepan. Cover with the water and add the peeled garlic clove, bay leaf, and ¼ onion.

2. Bring the water to a boil over medium-high heat, then reduce the heat to a simmer. Cook for about 40 minutes, until the meat is tender and the water has reduced. At this point, the meat will start to brown in its own fat.

3. Meanwhile, preheat a comal or large skillet over medium-high heat, then roast the tomatillos, peppers, and the remaining ⅓ onion and 2 unpeeled garlic cloves. (See page 16 for specific roasting instructions for each vegetable.) Wrap all the roasted vegetables in a large piece of aluminum foil so they keep cooking in their own steam for about 5 minutes.

4. Place the roasted vegetables and chopped cilantro in a blender, and blend until smooth.

5. Once the meat is cooked and slightly browned, add the vegetable oil. Once the oil is hot, pour the sauce into the saucepan, season with the salt and pepper, and bring to a boil. Stir in the nopales, then reduce the heat to simmer for 7 to 8 minutes.

6. Serve with the rice and tortillas.

NOTA *You can add an avocado leaf along with the bay leaf when cooking the meat. This will add a more herbaceous flavor to the meat.*

ENSALADA DE POLLO

Chicken Salad

The chicken salad that is made in Mexico is an adaption of the famous Russian Olivier salad, but with chicken added. Some variations include other ingredients, like red peppers and corn. It is a classic party dish that continues to be popular throughout Mexico.

PREP TIME: 15 minutes plus 4 hours chilling time	**YIELD:** 8 servings

1 pound (450 g) chicken breast, cooked and shredded

14 ounces (400 g) potatoes, cooked and diced

8 ounces (225 g) carrots, cooked and diced

5 ounces (140 g) celery, diced

6 ounces (170 g) canned sweet peas, drained

1 Golden or Red Delicious apple, peeled and diced

1 cup (225 g) mayonnaise

Salt and pepper, to taste

GARNISHING AND TO SERVE

1 sprig fresh parsley

Saltines

Pickled jalapeños and carrot slices

1. Place the shredded chicken in a large bowl with the potatoes, carrots, celery, sweet peas, and apple. Gently mix together and stir in the mayonnaise. Do this carefully to avoid breaking up or mashing the cooked vegetables.

2. Season the salad with the salt and pepper, then refrigerate for about 4 hours to allow the flavors to blend.

3. Garnish with the parsley and serve with the saltines and pickled jalapeños and carrot slices (for the adults).

NOTAS

* *The addition of the apple is something I started doing many years ago, though it is not very common in Mexico.*

* *You can refrigerate this salad for up to 2 days.*

ENSALADA DE CODITOS

Macaroni Salad

Also known as *sopa fría* (cold soup), this macaroni salad is most often served alongside Ensalada de Pollo (opposite), as the two complement each other well. In the state of Sinaloa, it is a favorite side dish for parties, where it's served with Barbacoa de Lengua (page 53) and Asado de Puerco (page 66). In my hometown of Tampico, in the state of Tamaulipas, this dish and the chicken salad are both often seen on the menu at children's birthday parties, served with a generous portion of saltine crackers and some pickled jalapeños and carrots for the adults.

PREP TIME: 10 minutes plus 4 hours chilling time	**COOK TIME:** 12 minutes	**YIELD:** 8 servings

8 ounces (225 g) elbow macaroni

10 ounces (280 g) American or Cheddar cheese, cut into squares or cubes

10 ounces (280 g) cooked ham, cut into small cubes

1½ cups (360 ml) Mexican crema or sour cream

¼ cup (55 g) mayonnaise

Salt and pepper, to taste

1 sprig fresh parsley, for garnishing

1. Cook the macaroni according to the package directions, then drain and set aside to cool.

2. Place the cheese and ham in a large bowl, then stir in the cooled macaroni (make sure the macaroni is cool; otherwise, its heat will cause the cheese to melt).

3. In a smaller bowl, mix the Mexican crema with the mayonnaise, salt, and pepper. Gently fold this mixture into the bowl with the macaroni, ham, and cheese, and thoroughly coat all the ingredients. Refrigerate until chilled, about 4 hours.

4. To serve, garnish the macaroni salad with the parsley.

NOTAS

✖ *Some recipes add diced celery, corn, peas, and other vegetables to this salad. If you choose to use them, add them with the cheese and ham in step 2.*

✖ *You can refrigerate this salad for up to 3 days.*

FILETE DE PESCADO EMPANIZADO

Breaded Fish Fillet

When you grow up in a seaport like my hometown of Tampico, seafood will be an essential part of your weekly menu. To make this recipe, my mom would use catfish or tilapia. You can use different types of fish, as long as you take into account how well the fish holds its shape while frying. Ask your local fishmonger for their recommendations.

PREP TIME: 15 minutes	**COOK TIME:** 20 minutes	**YIELD:** 6 servings

2¼ pounds (1 kg) tilapia (6 fillets)

1 tablespoon (15 ml) fresh lime juice

Salt and pepper, to taste

½ teaspoon onion powder

½ teaspoon garlic powder

2 large eggs

2 cups (200 g) dried bread crumbs or crushed saltines

¾ cup (180 ml) vegetable oil

GARNISHING AND TO SERVE

Arroz Blanco (page 130) or Arroz Rojo (page 132)

Green salad of your choice

Lime wedges

Warm corn tortillas

Spicy salsa of your choice

NOTAS

* *If you use saltines, make sure to adjust the salt accordingly, as the crackers have salt in them.*

* *You can freeze breaded fillets (uncooked) for up to 6 weeks. Wrap each fillet in plastic wrap, then place them in a freezer bag. Thaw before frying.*

1. Pat the fish fillets dry. Sprinkle with the lime juice and season with the salt, pepper (freshly ground, if possible), and onion and garlic powders.

2. Beat the eggs in a large bowl, then place the fish in the egg mixture.

3. Spread the bread crumbs on a large dish. Have another large plate ready to place the fish on after breading them.

4. Using kitchen tongs or your hands, place a fish fillet in the bread crumbs, turn to coat the other side, and turn again if needed until the fillet is well coated. Lightly pat down on the crumbs to ensure that they adhere to the surface of the fish. Place the breaded fillet on the clean plate and repeat this process with the remaining fillets.

5. Heat the oil in a large skillet over medium-high heat. Line a plate with paper towels. Once the oil is hot, place the breaded fillets in the pan. You can fry 2 or 3 fillets at a time, just make sure not to overcrowd the pan. Cook for 3 to 4 minutes per each side until they are golden, then place them on a prepared plate to drain any excess oil.

6. Serve with the rice, salad, lime wedges, tortillas, and salsa.

FRIJOL CON PUERCO

Pork and Beans

This dish is from the state of Yucatán, but it is also loved in nearby states such as Campeche, Quintana Roo, and Tabasco. One of the first things I learned when I moved to Tabasco was that Mondays were Frijol con Puerco Day. Now I understand why. Monday was laundry day, and back then, the women had to spend long hours doing the laundry by hand. The ease of making a simple stew allowed them to dedicate their time to other chores while the food simmered in the kitchen. This custom continues to this day, as many eateries and restaurants serve this dish on Mondays. This is one of those dishes that tastes better when reheated, so double this recipe and freeze some for later.

PREP TIME: 15 minutes	**COOK TIME:** 1 hour 20 minutes	**YIELD:** 6 servings

1 cup (240 g) dried black beans

4 cups (1 quart/950 ml) water

1 clove garlic

¼ white onion

2 pounds (900 g) pork shoulder, cut into 2-inch (5 cm) cubes

1 small sprig epazote

Salt, to taste

GARNISHING AND TO SERVE

6 small radishes, chopped

½ cup (20 g) chopped fresh cilantro

⅓ cup (40 g) chopped white onion

Lime wedges (optional)

Chiltomate salsa (optional) (see Notas)

Arroz Blanco (page 130)

1. Before cooking the beans, check to see if there are any broken or dried-up ones and remove them. Rinse the beans and place them in a large stockpot or casserole. Cover with the water and add the garlic and onion. Remove any beans that float to the surface, as these are probably too old and damaged.

2. Place the pot over high heat and bring to a boil, then reduce the heat to a simmer. Partially cover the pot to allow some of the steam to be released. Cook the beans for about 40 minutes, then add the pork and epazote, and season with the salt. Continue cooking for another 40 to 45 minutes, until the meat and beans are tender. If the broth reduces too much, add about ¼ cup (60 ml) hot water. Taste the stew to see if it needs more salt.

3. Serve in large bowls and place the garnishes and rice in serving dishes for everyone to customize their own.

NOTAS

* If using an Instant Pot, cook the beans for 15 minutes, then release the pressure valve, add the pork, and cook for another 15 to 20 minutes. If you using a slow cooker, cook the beans on the low setting for 3 hours, then add the pork and continue cooking for 3 more hours.

* This dish tastes even better when it's made with pork ribs, so replace half the pork shoulder with ribs to enhance the flavors.

* To make the chiltomate salsa, place 2 plum tomatoes, 2 onion slices (½ inch/ 1 cm thick), and 1 habanero pepper in a hot skillet. Cook them evenly, about 8 minutes, and remove promptly. Make a smooth salsa using a molcajete or a blender, adding a little bit of water if needed.

PICADILLO

The name *picadillo* comes from the Spanish verb *picar*, which means "to chop or mince," and most of the ingredients in this dish are chopped. Picadillo is prepared in many Latin American countries with several variations, but in essence, it is a comfort food comprised of ground beef, tomato sauce, and vegetables. It is a very flexible dish, and you can change the ingredients to make a picadillo you can call your own. Picadillo is also used as a filling for gorditas and burritos and as a topping for sopes. My son even likes to make sandwiches with picadillo, which are similar to Sloppy Joes!

PREP TIME: 15 minutes	**COOK TIME:** 30 minutes	**YIELD:** 6 servings

2 tablespoons (30 ml) vegetable oil

1 pound (450 g) ground beef

½ large onion, finely chopped

2 cloves garlic, minced

1 cup (120 g) diced carrots (about 2 medium carrots)

1 cup (140 g) diced potatoes (about 2 small potatoes)

2 medium tomatoes, coarsely chopped

½ cup (120 ml) water

1 cup (145 g) green peas (if canned, drain, and if frozen, thaw)

Salt and pepper, to taste

TO SERVE

Arroz Rojo (page 132) or Arroz Blanco (page 130)

Warm corn tortillas

1. Heat the oil in a large skillet over medium-high heat. Add the ground beef and cook for 5 minutes, using a spatula or wooden spoon to break up any large pieces.

2. Stir in the onion and garlic, and continue cooking until the onion is slightly translucent, about 2 minutes. Add the carrots and cook for about 5 more minutes. Then add the potatoes and continue cooking for 5 more minutes, stirring frequently.

3. While the meat and vegetables are cooking, place the tomatoes and water in a blender, and blend until smooth. Add this sauce to the skillet and stir in the peas.

4. Season with the salt and pepper, and simmer until the vegetables are cooked and the liquid has reduced, about 10 minutes. If the liquid reduces before the vegetables are cooked, add about ¼ cup (60 ml) of water and continue cooking.

5. Serve with the rice and tortillas.

NOTAS

* Raisins, olives, and capers are other ingredients some cooks add to their picadillo. Add in step 3 with the sauce and peas.

* The amount of picadillo this recipe makes is enough for stuffing 8 poblano peppers for making Chiles Rellenos (page 55).

POLLO A LA VERACRUZANA

Chicken Veracruz-Style

I've been making this stew for years, but without using a recipe. The way I grew up cooking was adding a little bit of this, a pinch of that, and tasting to see if it needed something else. This is a very forgiving dish, allowing you to use vegetables you have on hand in your kitchen.

PREP TIME: 10 minutes	COOK TIME: 50 minutes	YIELD: 6 servings

2 tablespoons (30 ml) olive oil

6 bone-in, skin-on chicken thighs, whole, or 3 breasts, cut in half

Salt and pepper, to taste

½ medium white onion, finely chopped

4 cloves garlic, minced

2 carrots, diced

1 large potato, diced

1 pound (450 g) chopped tomatoes

1 cup (240 ml) water

1 bay leaf

½ teaspoon dried thyme or a small fresh sprig

½ teaspoon marjoram (optional)

⅓ cup (40 g) pimento-stuffed olives, sliced

¼ cup (35 g) raisins

2 teaspoons capers

TO SERVE

Arroz Blanco (page 130)

Pickled jalapeño peppers

1. Heat the oil in a large skillet over medium-high heat. Season the chicken with the salt and pepper, then add it to the skillet and sear for 7 to 8 minutes per side. Once the chicken is browned, remove it from the pan and set aside (somewhere it will stay warm).

2. Add the onion to the skillet and cook for about 2 minutes, then stir in the garlic and carrots and cook for 5 minutes. Add the potatoes and cook for 2 more minutes.

3. Place the chopped tomatoes and water into a blender, and blend until smooth. Pour the tomato sauce into the skillet, using a strainer.

4. Return the chicken to the skillet, bring the sauce to a boil over medium-high heat, and then reduce the heat to a simmer. Add the bay leaf, thyme, marjoram (if using), olives, raisins, and capers. Season with salt and pepper and cover. Simmer until the chicken and vegetables are cooked, 10 to 12 minutes. The cooking time will vary depending on the size and type of chicken pieces.

5. Serve with the rice and pickled jalapeño peppers.

NOTAS

* This stew uses many ingredients, but all of them add up to the richness of its flavor. Some people eliminate the carrots and potatoes, while others add the vegetables available in their region or in season. Sometimes I even add a little bit of wine and some sweet peas too.

* If the fresh tomatoes you're using don't have enough juice, simply add a few teaspoons of tomato paste to the sauce.

* During the winter, I make this stew using canned whole tomatoes.

TINGA DE POLLO

Chicken Tinga

Chicken tinga is originally from the state of Puebla, but this recipe is for the version that is the most popular throughout all of Mexico. I love to eat this tinga as a topping for corn tostadas, but it can also be used as a taco filling, as well as a dish you can serve with a side of rice and a salad. It is also a popular stuffing for fried corn empanadas and a topping for sopes.

PREP TIME: 10 minutes	**COOK TIME:** 25 minutes	**YIELD:** 6 servings

2 tablespoons (30 ml) vegetable oil

1 medium white onion, sliced

2 large cloves garlic, minced

3 cups (500 g) diced tomato

2 tablespoons (6 g) chopped fresh parsley

3 cups (450 g) cooked and shredded chicken

2 chipotle peppers in adobo sauce (from a can), chopped

Salt and pepper, to taste

GARNISHING AND TO SERVE

Chopped fresh parsley

Corn tostadas (optional)

1. Heat the oil in a large skillet over medium heat and add the onion. Stir-fry for 3 minutes, then stir in the garlic. Cook for another 2 minutes until fragrant.

2. Add the tomato and parsley, reduce the heat, stir, and cook until the tomatoes start releasing their juices, 6 to 7 minutes. If your tomatoes aren't juicy enough, add a couple tablespoons (30 ml) of water. Add the chicken and chipotle peppers. Simmer for about 8 more minutes, until all the flavors have blended together. Season the chicken with the salt and pepper.

3. Garnish with the chopped parsley and serve with the tostadas (if using).

NOTAS

* *You can use store-bought rotisserie chicken to prepare this dish. You can also prepare tinga with pork and beef.*

* *Adjust the amount of chipotle peppers you use depending on how spicy you want the tinga to be.*

* *If you have leftovers, they can be stored in the freezer for about a month.*

POLLO EN SALSA VERDE CON CALABACITAS

Chicken with Squash in Green Salsa

This recipe is one of the many ways you can use tomatillos, which are also known as *tomates verdes*. For this recipe, I added Mexican squash, but you can add zucchini, chayotes, green beans, and other green vegetables. The addition of vegetables to this dish is widespread in Mexico; it adds more flavor and texture to the stew, and it's a great way to eat your daily amount of veggies.

PREP TIME: 20 minutes	**COOK TIME:** 40 minutes	**YIELD:** 4 servings

4 skin-on, bone-in chicken thighs

Salt and pepper, to taste

¼ whole plus ¼ chopped medium white onion, divided

2 cloves garlic, divided

2 sprigs fresh cilantro, divided

1 pound (450 g) tomatillos (about 11 medium tomatillos), husks removed

2 serrano peppers or 1 jalapeño pepper

1½ tablespoons (22 ml) vegetable oil

8 ounces (225 g) Mexican squash or zucchini, diced

TO SERVE

Arroz Rojo (page 132) (optional)

Warm corn tortillas (optional)

NOTA *Some people like this stew to be served more like a soup, in which case they would add more of the broth. The quantity added depends on how soupy they want the dish to be.*

1. Season the chicken pieces with the salt, then place them in a stockpot with the ¼ whole onion, 1 garlic clove, and 1 cilantro sprig. Cover with water, place over high heat, and bring to a boil. Reduce the heat and simmer gently for 30 minutes, or until the chicken is cooked and soft. Remove from the heat and drain, reserving the chicken broth and discarding the onion, garlic, and cilantro. Set aside.

2. While the chicken is cooking, place the tomatillos, remaining garlic clove, and serrano peppers in a separate large saucepan, cover with water, and cook for 15 minutes over medium heat.

3. Transfer the tomatillos, garlic, and serrano peppers to a blender, and blend until smooth.

4. Heat the oil in a large skillet over medium-high heat. Add the remaining chopped onion and cook for 2 minutes. Stir in the squash and continue cooking for 4 minutes, then pour in the sauce and add the chicken. Let simmer for 10 minutes. If the sauce gets too thick, add about ½ cup (120 ml) of the reserved chicken broth. Season with salt and pepper.

5. To serve, garnish with the remaining cilantro sprig and serve with the rice (if using) and the tortillas (if using).

POLLO ENTOMATADO

Chicken in Tomato Sauce

Pollo entomatado is a simple but flavorful dish. It doesn't need much in the way of spices or herbs to make it one of the most memorable stews you will ever taste. It is a homey dish, and I love to eat it with bread to soak up all those delicious tomato juices. For this dish, I try to buy the juiciest tomatoes in the market. I like to take advantage of summer tomatoes because they always produce a rich sauce.

PREP TIME: 15 minutes	**COOK TIME:** 45 minutes	**YIELD:** 4 servings

4 pieces skin-on, bone-in chicken (about 2 pounds/900 g) (see Notas)

Salt and pepper, to taste

2 tablespoons (30 ml) vegetable oil

¼ cup (30 g) chopped white onion

1 small clove garlic, diced

1 poblano pepper, diced

1 jalapeño pepper, diced

1½ pounds (680 g) chopped fresh tomatoes

1 cup (240 ml) water

GARNISHING AND TO SERVE

¼ cup (10 g) chopped fresh parsley or cilantro

Arroz Blanco (page 130)

1. Season the chicken with the salt and pepper. Set aside.

2. Heat the oil in a large stockpot or Dutch oven over medium-high heat. Add the chicken pieces, skin sides down. Cook the chicken, turning once, until both sides are golden brown, about 10 minutes.

3. Reduce the heat to medium and stir in the onion and garlic. Cook for about 3 minutes, until the onion looks transparent. Add the peppers and continue cooking for 5 more minutes. Using a wooden spoon, scrape away any browned bits at the bottom of the pot. Stir in the chopped tomatoes and cook for 5 more minutes.

4. Add the water, increase the heat to medium-high, and bring to a boil. Reduce the heat to a simmer, cover, and cook for 25 to 30 minutes, or until the chicken is cooked and tender. Taste and season with salt.

5. Garnish with the chopped parsley or cilantro and serve with the rice.

NOTAS

* *For this recipe, I used 1 chicken thigh, 1 chicken leg, and 1 chicken breast cut into two pieces.*

* *Add more jalapeño peppers if you want more heat.*

* *Some cooks also add 1 chicken bouillon cube with the water in step 4 to enhance the flavor of this dish.*

ROPA VIEJA

Shredded Beef in Tomato Sauce

Ropa vieja, which means "old clothes" in Spanish, is a dish that is found throughout many Latin American countries, including Mexico. This stew consists of shredded beef cooked with vegetables in a tomato-based broth. Whenever I make Caldo de Res (page 28), I like to cook extra meat so I can make this dish later in the week.

PREP TIME: 15 minutes	COOK TIME: 2 hours 10 minutes	YIELD: 6 servings

BEEF

1½ pounds (675 g) skirt steak, flank steak, or rump roast, cut into large cubes

⅓ medium white onion

4 large cloves garlic

1 bay leaf

STEW

3 large tomatoes

2 cloves garlic

2 tablespoons (30 ml) vegetable oil

¾ white onion, thinly sliced

2 medium potatoes, cut into bite-size cubes

1 bay leaf

1 teaspoon dried Mexican oregano

⅓ teaspoon freshly ground cumin seeds

2 pickled jalapeño peppers, sliced

1 tablespoon (15 ml) vinegar from the jalapeño peppers (optional)

Salt and pepper, to taste

TO SERVE

Arroz Blanco (page 130)

Frijoles de la Olla (page 138) (optional)

Warm corn tortillas

1. To make the beef: Place the meat, onion, garlic, and bay leaf in a large stockpot, then fill it with enough water to cover the meat. Place the pot over high heat and bring to a boil. Reduce the heat to low, cover, and simmer for 2 to 3 hours, until the meat is tender enough to shred. Remove the meat from the pot and let cool until you can handle it, then shred it and set aside. Reserve at least 1 cup (240 ml) of the cooking broth to use for the stew.

2. While the meat is cooking, make the stew: Place the tomatoes and garlic in a large saucepan and cover with water. Turn the heat to medium-high and bring to a boil. Reduce the heat to medium-low, cover, and cook until the tomatoes are tender and the skins are peeling, about 15 minutes. Set the pan aside to cool slightly.

3. Heat the oil in a large skillet over medium-high heat. Add the onion and cook for 1 minute, then add the diced potatoes and cook for 5 more minutes, stirring frequently to keep them from sticking to the pan.

4. While the potatoes are cooking and the tomatoes have cooled a little, remove the skins from the tomatoes and place them in a blender with the garlic cloves. Blend until smooth (there's no need to add water).

5. Add the tomato sauce, the 1 cup (240 ml) reserved beef broth, and 1 bay leaf to the skillet with the onion and potatoes. Stir and continue cooking for another 5 minutes, then reduce the heat to low and add the shredded meat. Cook for 8 to 10 more minutes.

6. Check the potatoes for doneness, ensuring they are keeping their shape and don't overcook. Stir in the oregano and cumin, along with the jalapeño slices and their vinegar (if using). Season with the salt and pepper. The stew is ready when the potatoes are tender and all the flavors have blended.

7. Serve with the rice, beans (if using), and tortillas.

NOTAS

❋ *You can also cook the meat in an Instant Pot or pressure cooker for 45 minutes and in a slow cooker on the low setting for 8 hours.*

❋ *You can omit the jalapeños or add more if you like. You can also substitute fresh jalapeños.*

❋ *Sometimes I add sliced pimento-stuffed olives and a teaspoon of chopped capers to this dish, because that's the way my husband likes it. Add in step 6 with the jalapeños.*

TAMALES DE POLLO EN SALSA VERDE

Chicken in Green Salsa Tamales

These tamales are among the most popular tamales in Mexico, particularly in the center of the country. They are also one of the most commonly known tamales in the United States, along with Tamales de Puerco (page 113). The word *tamal* comes from the Nahuatl word *tamalli*, meaning "wrapped." Tamales are steamed in a leaf wrapper, usually a corn husk or a banana leaf, but other wrappers include avocado leaves, hoja santa, and other nontoxic leaves found in Mexico.

PREP TIME: 40 minutes	**COOK TIME:** 1 hour 40 minutes	**YIELD:** 36 tamales

CHICKEN

1½ pounds (675 g) boneless, skinless chicken breasts

2 thick slices onion

2 cloves garlic

SALSA

1½ pounds (675 g) tomatillos, husks removed

6 serrano peppers or 4 jalapeño peppers

2 cloves garlic

Salt, to taste

DOUGH

36 medium corn husks, plus 10 more for lining the steaming pot

1¾ cups (360 g) lard

5 cups (615 g) masa harina for tamales

1 teaspoon baking powder

6 cups (1½ quarts/1.4 L) warm chicken broth, plus more if needed

Salt, to taste

1. To make the chicken: Place the chicken, onion, and garlic in a large stockpot. Cover the ingredients with water and cook over medium heat for 40 minutes, until the chicken is tender. Remove the chicken, let it cool, and then shred it with two forks.

2. While the chicken is cooking, make the salsa: Place the tomatillos, peppers, and garlic in a large pot with enough water to cover the ingredients. Cook, covered, over medium heat until they are cooked and tender, 15 to 18 minutes.

3. Transfer the tomatillos, peppers, and garlic to a blender, and blend until smooth. Season the sauce with the salt and mix with the shredded chicken. Set aside.

4. To make the dough: Place all the corn husks in a large bowl with warm water to soak for about 30 minutes; this will help make the husks soft and easily pliable when preparing the tamales. Remove the husks, drain any excess water, and set aside.

5. Place the lard in a large bowl and begin to beat it by hand or with a hand mixer until it acquires a lighter color and a slightly fluffy texture. Slowly incorporate the masa harina, baking powder, and warm broth. Continue mixing until all the ingredients are well incorporated, then season with the salt. If the dough looks too dry, add a little bit more broth to it, a couple tablespoons (30 ml) at a time.

(continued)

6. To assemble the tamales, place a corn husk on your work surface with the wide end facing toward you. Place 2 to 3 tablespoons (15 to 30 g) of the dough in the center of the corn husk, closer to the bottom of the husk (the wide end). Using the back of a large spoon, evenly spread the dough toward the left, right, and bottom edges. The dough should reach all the way to the bottom edge (or just before it) but leave an inch (2.5 cm) of space on the left and right sides. Top the dough with 2 tablespoons (38 g) of the chicken filling. Fold the right and left sides of the corn husk in toward the center, overlapping each other and completely covering the dough and the filling. Next, fold the narrow end of the husk up toward the center. Repeat this process for the remaining 35 husks, dough, and filling. I usually line up the formed tamales on a tray as I make them.

7. To steam the tamales, place a steamer rack inside a large stockpot. Add enough warm water so that it almost reaches the steamer rack, then line the rack with a layer of corn husks. Place the tamales in the pot in an upright position, with the open ends facing up. Cover them with a generous layer of husks, then cover the pot. Steam the tamales for about 1 hour over medium heat. During the steaming, check the pot to see if it has enough water (be careful when removing the lid), adding more if needed (see Notas). To check if the tamales are ready, remove one from the pot, wait 5 minutes, then open it. If the husk separates easily from the dough when you open it, that means that the tamal is ready. If the dough sticks to the husk, place it back in the pot and cook for 15 more minutes.

8. Serve the tamales while still hot; just let them rest for 5 minutes first so the dough can firm up.

NOTAS

* *Instead of the lard, you can use shortening or even vegetable oil.*

* *To beat the dough, I usually use a hand mixer, but I use a stand mixer when making a large batch of dough.*

* *When assembling tamales, cooks do not actually measure out the specific amounts of dough and filling that are added to every husk. Instead, they spoon on the amounts that they deem appropriate, while trying to stay within a consistent range. The amounts used can depend on how much area the corn husk has (they may vary in size), as well as how large the cook wants the tamales to be.*

* *You can tie the tamales with a strip of corn husk. It is not necessary, but it does help to keep them intact during the cooking process (this is especially true when making larger tamales). Some people use the strip as an indicator when making different types of tamales, only tying one type so that it's easy to tell which is which without having to open them.*

* *If you need to add more water to the pot when steaming the tamales, make sure to pour it as close to the wall of the pot as possible, avoiding the tamales. If water gets into the tamales, they will lose their flavor and the dough will be soggy.*

* *One trick Mexican cooks use is to place a coin at the bottom of the pot underneath the steaming rack. If the water evaporates, the coin will start rattling, letting you know that you need to add more water to the pot.*

* *Tamales can be frozen in plastic bags for up to 4 months. You can reheat frozen tamales in the microwave for 2 minutes per tamal if they are frozen and 1 minute if they are thawed, re-steam thawed tamales for 15 minutes, or place thawed tamales, with the corn husks still on, in a skillet over medium-high heat for 10 minutes. The corn husks will start roasting, which will add an extra smoky flavor to the tamales. Turn them 2 or 3 times until warm.*

TAMALES DE PUERCO

Pork Tamales

These tamales are filled with pork in a sauce made with dried red peppers. They are very similar to the tamales made in the northern states of Coahuila, Tamaulipas, and Nuevo Leon. A woman from Monclova in Coahuila, named Yolanda, gave me this recipe years ago. She prepared these tamales to sell to her neighbors every weekend, and I always think of her when making them.

PREP TIME: 45 minutes	**COOK TIME:** 2 hours 15 minutes	**YIELD:** 16 tamales

PORK

1 pound (450 g) pork shoulder, cut into cubes

2 cloves garlic

¼ white onion

1 bay leaf

1 teaspoon salt

4 cups (1 quart/950 ml) water

SALSA

2 ancho peppers, sliced open, seeded, and veins removed

3 guajillo peppers, sliced open, seeded, and veins removed

2 small cloves garlic

⅓ teaspoon ground cumin

1 tablespoon (15 ml) vegetable oil

Salt and black pepper, to taste

DOUGH

16 large corn husks, plus 10 more for lining the steaming pot

1⅓ cups (275 g) lard

3 cups (370 g) masa harina

1 teaspoon baking powder

Salt, if needed

1. To make the pork: In a medium pot, combine the pork, garlic, onion, bay leaf, and salt. Cover with the water. Bring to a boil over medium-high heat, then reduce the heat. Simmer, partially covered, occasionally using a large spoon to skim off any foam that forms on the surface, for about 1 hour, or until the meat is tender enough to shred. Remove and discard the onion, garlic, and bay leaf. When the meat is cool enough to handle, shred into bite-size pieces with two forks. Set aside. Reserve the cooking broth to use for the salsa and the dough.

2. While the meat is cooking, make the salsa: Soak the dried peppers in a medium bowl with warm water for about 20 minutes. Drain the peppers, reserving the water, and place them in a blender, along with the garlic, cumin, and ⅓ cup (75 ml) of the reserved soaking water. Blend until smooth.

3. Heat the vegetable oil in a large skillet over medium heat, then add the salsa with 1 cup (240 ml) of the reserved pork broth and cook for 8 minutes. Add the shredded pork to the sauce and season with the salt and pepper. Add more pork broth if the meat becomes dry. Simmer until heated through, about 5 more minutes.

4. To make the dough: Place all the corn husks in a large bowl with warm water to soak for about 30 minutes; this will help make the husks soft and easily pliable when preparing the tamales. Remove the husks, drain any excess water, and set aside.

5. Place the lard in a large bowl and begin to beat it by hand or with a hand mixer until it acquires a lighter color and a slightly fluffy texture. Slowly incorporate the masa harina, baking powder, and

(continued)

2½ cups (600 ml) reserved warm pork broth. Continue mixing until all the ingredients are well incorporated, then season with the salt. If the dough looks too dry, add a little bit more broth to it, a couple tablespoons (30 ml) at a time.

6. To assemble the tamales, place a corn husk on your work surface with the wide end facing toward you. Place 2 tablespoons (30 g) of the dough in the center of the corn husk, closer to the bottom of the husk (the wide end). Using the back of a large spoon, evenly spread the dough toward the left, right, and bottom edges. The dough should reach all the way to the bottom edge (or just before it) but leave an inch (2.5 cm) of space on the left and right sides. Top the dough with 1½ tablespoons (27 g) of the meat filling. Fold the right and left sides of the corn husk in toward the center, overlapping each other and completely covering the dough and the filling. Next, fold the narrow end of the husk up toward the center. Repeat this process for the remaining 15 husks, dough, and filling. I usually line up the formed tamales on a tray as I make them.

7. To steam the tamales, place a steamer rack inside a large stockpot. Add enough warm water so that it almost reaches the steamer rack, then line the rack with a layer of corn husks. Place the tamales in the pot in an upright position, with the open ends facing up. Cover them with a generous layer of husks, then cover the pot. Steam the tamales for about 1 hour over medium heat. During the steaming, check the pot to see if it has enough water (be careful when removing the lid), adding more if needed (see Notas). To check if the tamales are ready, remove one from the pot, wait 5 minutes, then open it. If the husk separates easily from the dough when you open it, that means that the tamal is ready. If the dough sticks to the husk, place it back in the pot and cook for 15 more minutes.

8. Serve the tamales while still hot; just let them rest for 5 minutes so the dough can firm up.

NOTAS

* *Instead of the lard, you can use shortening or even vegetable oil.*

* *When assembling tamales, cooks do not actually measure out the specific amounts of dough and filling that are added to every husk. Instead, they spoon on the amounts that they deem appropriate, while trying to stay within a consistent range. The amounts used can depend on how much area the corn husk has (they may vary in size), as well as how large the cook wants the tamales to be.*

* *If you need to add more water to the pot when steaming the tamales, make sure to pour it as close to the wall of the pot as possible, avoiding the tamales. If water gets into the tamales, they will lose their flavor and the dough will be soggy.*

* *Tamales can be frozen in plastic bags for up to 4 months. You can reheat frozen tamales in the microwave for 2 minutes per tamal if they are frozen and 1 minute if they are thawed, re-steam thawed tamales for 15 minutes, or place thawed tamales, with the corn husks still on, in a skillet over medium-high heat for 10 minutes. The corn husks will start roasting, which will add an extra smoky flavor to the tamales. Turn them 2 or 3 times until warm.*

TAMALES DE RAJAS CON QUESO

Cheese and Vegetable Tamales

Tamales de rajas con queso are a popular variety of tamal filled with tomato sauce, cheese, and strips of poblano peppers. The mellow flavor of the cheese is a perfect match for the spiciness and smokiness of the roasted peppers. You can serve these tamales by themselves or alongside other types of tamales to provide a meatless option for guests. These tamales are also known simply as *tamales de rajas*. The word *rajas* means "strips," and refers to the strips of poblano peppers.

PREP TIME: 40 minutes	**COOK TIME:** 1 hour 20 minutes	**YIELD:** 12 tamales

FILLING

2 large tomatoes

1 jalapeño or 2 serrano peppers, stemmed

1 small clove garlic, chopped

1 tablespoon (8 g) chopped white onion

2 poblano peppers

Salt, to taste

10 ounces (280 g) Oaxaca or panela cheese, cut into 1-inch-long (2.5 cm) strips

DOUGH

16 large corn husks, plus 10 more for lining the steaming pot

⅔ cup (135 g) lard

2 cups (245 g) masa harina

½ teaspoon baking powder

1¾ cups (420 ml) warm chicken broth

Salt, to taste

1. To make the filling: Place the tomatoes and jalapeño pepper in a saucepan and cover with water. Cook over medium-high heat until tender, 12 to 15 minutes. Drain the water, reserving a couple tablespoons (30 ml) in case you need it to thin the sauce in step 2.

2. Place the tomatoes and jalapeño pepper in a blender with the garlic and onion. Blend until smooth, then season with the salt. Set aside.

3. Roast the poblano peppers over an open flame of your stove over medium-high heat, turning for even roasting, 8 to 10 minutes. Place the roasted peppers in a plastic bag and close it, letting them steam for 5 minutes. Remove from the bag and scrape off the charred skin by rubbing your fingers on the surface of the peppers. Using a sharp knife, cut a slit along the length of the peppers and remove the seeds and veins.

4. To make the dough: Place all the corn husks in a large bowl with warm water to soak for about 30 minutes; this will help make the husks soft and easily pliable when preparing the tamales. Drain and set aside.

5. Place the lard in a large bowl and begin to beat it by hand or with a hand mixer until it acquires a lighter color and a slightly fluffy texture. Slowly incorporate the masa harina, baking powder, and warm broth. Continue mixing until all the ingredients are well incorporated, then season with the salt. If the dough looks too dry, add a little bit more broth to it, a couple tablespoons (30 ml) at a time.

(continued)

6. To assemble the tamales, place a corn husk on your work surface with the wide end facing toward you. Place about 3 tablespoons (45 g) of the dough in the center of the bottom half of the corn husk. Evenly spread the dough, about ⅛ inch (3 mm) thick, with a large spoon to the bottom edge and leaving about an inch (2.5 cm) on the left and right sides. Add 1 tablespoon (15 ml) of the sauce, then top with some of the cheese and pepper strips (at least one of each). Fold the right and left sides of the corn husk in toward the center, overlapping and completely covering the dough and the filling. Fold up the narrow end of the husk toward the center, then tie the tamal using a thin strip of corn husk (tying is optional). Repeat this process with the remaining 11 corn husks, dough, sauce, and cheese and peppers.

7. To steam the tamales, place a steamer rack inside a large stockpot. Add enough warm water so that it almost reaches the steamer rack, then line the rack with a layer of corn husks. Place the tamales in the pot in an upright position, with the open ends facing up. Cover them with a generous layer of husks, then cover the pot. Steam the tamales for about 1 hour over medium heat. During the steaming, check the pot to see if it has enough water (be careful when removing the lid), adding more if needed (see Notas). To check if the tamales are ready, remove one from the pot, wait 5 minutes, then open it. If the husk separates easily from the dough when you open it, that means that the tamal is ready. If the dough sticks to the husk, place it back in the pot and cook for 15 more minutes.

8. Serve the tamales while still hot; just let them rest for 5 minutes so the dough can firm up. Servewith extra tomato sauce on top.

NOTAS

* *You can also use Salsa Verde (page 125) for the sauce. Make extra salsa for serving along with the cooked tamales. Some cooks prefer to use serrano or jalapeño peppers instead of the poblano peppers. If you can't find Oaxaca or panela cheese, substitute Monterey Jack or another type of cheese.*

* *Instead of the lard, you can use shortening or even vegetable oil.*

* *When assembling tamales, cooks do not actually measure out the specific amounts of dough and filling that are added to every husk. Instead, they spoon on the amounts that they deem appropriate, while trying to stay within a consistent range. The amounts used can depend on how much area the corn husk has (they may vary in size), as well as how large the cook wants the tamales to be.*

* *If you need to add more water to the pot when steaming the tamales, make sure to pour it as close to the wall of the pot as possible, avoiding the tamales. If water gets into the tamales, they will lose their flavor and the dough will be soggy.*

* *Tamales can be frozen in plastic bags for up to 4 months. You can reheat frozen tamales in the microwave for 2 minutes per tamal if they are frozen and 1 minute if they are thawed, re-steam thawed tamales for 15 minutes, or place thawed tamales, with the corn husks still on, in a skillet over medium-high heat for 10 minutes. The corn husks will start roasting, which will add an extra smoky flavor to the tamales. Turn them 2 or 3 times until warm.*

SALSAS
& SIDES

PICO DE GALLO

Pico de gallo has got to be one of the most popular salsas outside of Mexico. In Mexico, we also like to call it *salsa Mexicana*, since it has the colors of the Mexican flag: green, white, and red. This salsa is often used with grilled chicken and grilled or fried fish. Its ingredients are also commonly found in many seafood cocktail recipes. These days, some cooks customize this salsa by adding pineapple or mango, along with other peppers, like habanero.

PREP TIME: 10 minutes	**YIELD:** 1 cup (255 g)

1 large ripe tomato or 2 medium ripe tomatoes, finely chopped

⅓ large onion, finely chopped

2 serrano peppers or 1 jalapeño pepper, finely chopped

⅓ cup (13 g) finely chopped fresh cilantro

Juice of ½ lime

Salt, to taste

1. Place the tomato, onion, and peppers in a medium bowl. Add the cilantro, lime juice, and salt, then gently mix until all the ingredients are coated with the lime juice.

2. You can eat immediately or cover and refrigerate for 30 minutes before serving in order to enhance the flavors.

NOTAS

✳ *You can prepare the ingredients ahead of time, storing them in the refrigerator in separate containers.*

✳ *This salsa can be refrigerated for up to 3 days. The consistency won't be the same as when it's fresh, but it will be acceptable.*

SALSA ROJA

Red Salsa

This is a table salsa that you will find in many homes in my hometown of Tampico, as well as in many homes throughout Mexico. It is easy to make and uses ingredients that almost everyone has in their kitchen. This multipurpose salsa can be enjoyed at every meal.

PREP TIME: 5 minutes	**COOK TIME:** 15 minutes	**YIELD:** 1¼ cups (300 ml)

2 medium tomatoes

1 jalapeño pepper or 2 serrano peppers, stemmed

1 small clove garlic, chopped

1 tablespoon (8 g) chopped white onion

Salt, to taste

NOTA *This salsa can be refrigerated for up to 3 days and frozen for up to 4 weeks. Heat the salsa before serving.*

1. Place the tomatoes and pepper in a saucepan and cover with water. Cook over medium-high heat until the ingredients are tender, 12 to 15 minutes. Drain the water, reserving ½ cup (120 ml) in case you need it later, depending on how juicy the tomatoes are.

2. Place the tomatoes and pepper in a blender, along with the garlic and onion. Blend until smooth. If the salsa looks dry, add some of the reserved water, a couple tablespoons (30 ml) at a time (this depends on the juiciness of the tomatoes).

3. Transfer the salsa to a bowl and season with the salt. If you want a thinner salsa, add some of the reserved water.

4. Before serving, stir well for a smooth and even texture.

SALSA ROJA ROSTIZADA

Roasted Red Salsa

The roasted flavors of this salsa pair well with grilled meats and Guacamole (page 129). But to be honest, it tastes great regardless of what you put it on. Just a couple spoonfuls over a warm, freshly made tortilla tastes delightful, and it is even better if you add some diced avocado.

PREP TIME: 5 minutes	**COOK TIME:** 15 minutes	**YIELD:** 1 cup (240 ml)

2 medium tomatoes

1 small clove garlic, unpeeled

3 serrano peppers

2 teaspoons vegetable oil

Salt, to taste

NOTAS

* *I usually don't add water to this salsa because the tomatoes will be juicy and soft from roasting them.*

* *This salsa is best eaten immediately, but it can be refrigerated for up to 3 days.*

1. Preheat a comal or large skillet over medium-high heat, then roast the tomatoes, garlic, and peppers, turning them so they can roast evenly. (See page 16 for specific roasting instructions for each vegetable.) Once roasted, peel the garlic.

2. Place the roasted vegetables in a blender and blend until desired consistency. If you have a molcajete, this is the time to use it, as this is the way this salsa is traditionally prepared.

3. Heat the oil in a skillet over medium heat and add the salsa. Simmer for about 5 minutes.

4. Season with the salt and serve in a bowl.

SALSA TAQUERA

Taqueria-Style Salsa

This salsa is made with tomatillos and árbol peppers, and can also be prepared with other spicy, dried peppers, like puya or piquín. Salsa taquera is usually spicy, but you can adjust the spiciness to suit your taste by reducing or increasing the amount of árbol peppers.

PREP TIME: 5 minutes	**COOK TIME:** 15 minutes	**YIELD:** 1 cup (240 ml)

2 medium tomatoes

⅓ medium white onion (optional)

2 medium or 3 small tomatillos, husks removed

2 cloves garlic, unpeeled

15 árbol peppers

Salt, to taste

NOTAS

* For a deep-red color, use more tomatoes than tomatillos.

* This salsa can be refrigerated for up to 4 days and frozen for up to 6 weeks

1. Preheat a comal or large skillet over medium-high heat, then roast the tomatoes, onions (if using), tomatillos, and garlic, turning them so they can roast evenly. Once roasted, peel the garlic and set aside. Add the árbol peppers to the hot pan and slightly roast them. (See page 16 for specific roasting instructions for each vegetable.)

2. Once the árbol peppers are roasted, add them to a blender with the roasted tomatoes, tomatillos, garlic, and onion. Blend until smooth. If your salsa is too thick, add a little bit of water.

3. Season with the salt and serve in a bowl.

SALSA VERDE

Green Salsa

A common sight in any *taqueria*, this salsa is usually served alongside tacos and pork carnitas. The ingredients in this salsa are also an important component in many dishes, especially those called *en salsa verde*. Some dishes made with this salsa include Enchiladas Verdes (page 88), Tamales de Pollo en Salsa Verde (page 109), and Chicharrón en Salsa Verde (page 74). In addition to tacos, you can also serve this salsa with tostadas, flautas, gorditas, and other Mexican street foods.

PREP TIME: 5 minutes	**COOK TIME:** 15 minutes	**YIELD:** 1½ cups (360 ml)

About 3 cups water (710 ml)

2 or 3 serrano peppers or 1 jalapeño pepper

6 medium tomatillos, husks removed

1 clove garlic

3 tablespoons (24 g) chopped white onion

¼ cup (10 g) chopped fresh cilantro (optional)

Salt, to taste

1. Bring the water to a boil in a medium saucepan. Add the peppers and tomatillos, reduce the heat, and simmer, uncovered, for 12 to 15 minutes. Drain the water, reserving ¼ cup (60 ml).

2. Add the peppers, tomatillos, garlic, onion, and cilantro (if using) to a blender, and blend until smooth. Add a small amount of the cooking water to achieve a saucier texture.

3. Season with the salt and serve in a bowl.

NOTAS

* *Fresh tomatillos are not always available, but you can use canned tomatillos instead.*

* *If you don't want to blend in the cilantro in step 2, you can add it when serving.*

* *This salsa can be refrigerated for up to 3 days and frozen for up to 6 weeks. Heat the salsa before serving. You can reheat it in the microwave for 1 to 2 minutes or in a small saucepan over medium-low heat for 5 minutes, or until warm.*

SALSA VERDE ROSTIZADA

Roasted Green Salsa

Roasted salsas always have an added flavor due to the charred skins of the ingredients. If you like grilling meat, this is an excellent salsa to make, since you can prepare the ingredients while you're cooking on the grill. This salsa pairs well with red meats and grilled or fried fish. You can also serve this salsa as an appetizer with warm corn tortillas, slices of avocado, and queso fresco, or as a snack with a side of tortilla chips.

PREP TIME: 7 minutes	COOK TIME: 8 minutes	YIELD: 1½ cups (360 ml)

8 ounces (200 g) tomatillos (about 6 medium tomatillos), husks removed

2 serrano peppers

2 thick slices white onion (about ¼ onion)

1 clove garlic, unpeeled

¼ cup (10 g) chopped fresh cilantro

Salt, to taste

1. Preheat a comal or large skillet over medium-high heat, then roast the tomatillos, peppers, onion slices, and garlic, turning them so they roast evenly. (See page 16 for specific roasting instructions for each vegetable.) Once roasted, peel the garlic.

2. Place the roasted vegetables in a blender and blend until it has a slightly chunky texture. Add about ¼ cup (60 ml) of water if the consistency is too thick. Add the cilantro and blend again until everything is well incorporated.

3. Season with the salt and serve in a bowl.

NOTAS

✱ *You can swap 1 jalapeño pepper for the 2 serrano peppers. You can also use habanero peppers for extra heat.*

✱ *If you want to make this salsa ahead of time, do not add the cilantro. Instead, add it at serving time as a garnish.*

✱ *This salsa is often served with diced avocado on top.*

✱ *This salsa is best eaten immediately, but it can be refrigerated for up to 3 days.*

SALSA VERDE CREMOSA

Creamy Avocado Tomatillo Salsa

This salsa is very simple and easy to prepare, and you can make it just before serving. It's great to serve with Carnitas (page 50), Tacos de Bistec (page 46), or any type of crispy tacos. The avocado tames the spiciness of the peppers a bit, making this an excellent salsa for those who aren't used to or don't like spicy foods.

PREP TIME: 10 minutes	**YIELD:** 1¼ cups (300 ml)

3 medium tomatillos, husks removed and chopped

About 2 tablespoons (16 g) chopped onion

2 serrano peppers or 1 jalapeño pepper, chopped

⅓ cup (75 ml) water, plus 1 to 2 tablespoons (15 to 30 ml) more, if needed

6 sprigs fresh cilantro, chopped

1 medium ripe avocado, halved and pitted

Salt, to taste

1. Place the tomatillos in a blender, along with the onion, peppers, and water. Blend to a coarse texture.

2. Add the cilantro and avocado. Blend again until it reaches desired consistency, either smooth and creamy or chunky.

3. Season with the salt and serve in a bowl.

NOTA *The acidity of the tomatillos allows this salsa to keep in the refrigerator for up to 4 days.*

GUACAMOLE

The word "guacamole" comes from the Nahuatl word *ahuacamulli*, a combination of the word *ahuacatl*, meaning "avocado," and *mulli*, meaning "sauce" or "stew." Guacamole is one of the easiest Mexican recipes you can make. It uses only a few ingredients, and pairs well with a variety of foods. You can serve it as an appetizer with crispy tortilla chips, as a topping for tostadas, or as a side dish for grilled meats and fried seafood. A guacamole is only as good as the avocados you use to make it. In order to make sure you select perfectly ripe avocados, look for those that have a dark green color. The skin should give a little when you gently press it. If an avocado is too firm, it means it's not ripe yet, and if it feels mushy, it means the avocado is past its prime.

PREP TIME: 10 minutes	**YIELD:** 4 servings

2 large ripe avocados

Salt, to taste

1 small tomato, diced

¼ medium white onion, diced

1 serrano pepper, finely chopped

2 tablespoons (6 g) chopped fresh cilantro

Tortilla chips, to serve (optional)

1. Using a sharp knife, cut the avocados in half, twist to separate the halves, then remove the pit using the tip of the knife.

2. Using a spoon, scoop out the avocado flesh and place it in a molcajete, or a bowl, then mash the avocado using the pestle. If using a bowl, mash the avocado with a fork or a potato masher. It's your decision whether you want it smooth or a little chunky.

3. Season with the salt, then gently mix in the rest of the ingredients using a spoon.

4. Serve immediately with the tortilla chips (if using).

NOTAS

* *In Mexico, people sometimes save the avocado pit and place it in the center of the guacamole. Some believe it slows down the oxidation process and keeps the avocado from turning brown; others just add it as a decoration.*

* *The peppers used for guacamole are commonly serrano or jalapeño, but you can also use habanero, fresh piquín, or any other pepper, depending on the selection.*

* *Some cooks like to add a few drops of lime juice to preserve the avocado and prevent oxidation, as well as to add some acidity to the guacamole.*

* *If you're not serving the guacamole right away, cover it with plastic wrap, making sure that the plastic is touching the surface of the guacamole; this will help keep it from turning brown. If part of the surface does turn brown, simply remove it with a spoon and discard it.*

ARROZ BLANCO

White Rice

This rice is a terrific accompaniment to dishes like Mole Poblano (page 57), Asado de Puerco (page 66), Costillas en Salsa Verde (page 91), and many other traditional Mexican stews. It also makes a nice, quick dinner with a fried egg on top and some fried plantains. The preparation of this rice varies from region to region, but the end result is the same.

PREP TIME: 15 minutes	**COOK TIME:** 35 minutes	**YIELD:** 6 servings

1 cup (270 g) long-grain white rice

3 tablespoons (24 g) chopped white onion

1 small clove garlic

½ cup (120 ml) cold water

2 tablespoons vegetable (30 ml) oil or lard (30 g)

1½ cups (360 ml) hot water

1 to 2 sprigs fresh parsley or cilantro (optional)

1 serrano pepper (optional)

A few drops fresh lime or lemon juice

Salt, to taste

1. Place the rice in a large heatproof bowl and add enough hot water to cover the rice. Stir once, then let stand for 15 minutes.

2. Meanwhile, place the onion, garlic, and ½ cup (120 ml) cold water in a blender, and blend until smooth. Set aside.

3. Drain the rice in a strainer, then rinse it under cold water until the water runs clear. Shake the strainer well to remove any excess water, as the rice needs to be as dry as possible. Set aside to continue drying.

4. Heat the oil in a large saucepan or cazuela over medium-high heat. Add the rice and fry, stirring constantly, until it becomes transparent, 4 to 5 minutes. Don't overbrown the rice. When it's done, carefully tip the pan to one side and use a spoon to remove the excess oil.

5. Add the onion and garlic mixture to the rice in the saucepan and stir. Add the 1½ cups (360 ml) hot water, along with the parsley (if using), serrano pepper (if using), and lime juice, and bring to a boil.

6. Once it comes to a boil, reduce the heat to low, season with the salt, and cover. Cook for 15 to 20 minutes. Once you cover the rice, it is important not to stir or touch it until it is cooked; otherwise, it will become mushy. The water should be absorbed almost completely, and the rice should look cooked and fluffy. Once the rice is cooked, remove from the heat and let stand, covered, for 10 to 15 minutes to let the rice continue steaming. Discard the parsley, lightly fluff the rice with a fork, and serve.

NOTAS

❋ Long-grain rice works best, as it renders a fluffy and moist end result. It has less starch content, so the grains of the cooked rice will not stick together, provided you rinse them well before cooking.

❋ Some people only rinse the rice. I've found that when you soak it, the grains are more tender and fluffier.

❋ Some cooks prefer to add the garlic, minced, and the chopped onion while cooking the rice in step 4, instead of processing them in the blender in step 2.

❋ You can use chicken broth instead of the hot water, or a chicken bouillon cube dissolved in water. Keep in mind that your rice won't be as white in color if you use this option.

ARROZ ROJO

Red Rice

Red rice is prepared almost every day in some Mexican homes. An essential side dish found on plates throughout the country, this red rice can accompany almost any meal. In my home, we sometimes like to enjoy a small bowl of red rice topped with slices of avocados or a fried egg.

PREP TIME: 15 minutes	**COOK TIME:** 35 minutes	**YIELD:** 6 servings

1½ cups (270 g) long-grain white rice

3 tablespoons vegetable oil (45 ml) or lard (45 g)

2 medium tomatoes, chopped

3 tablespoons (24 g) chopped white onion

1 clove garlic, chopped

2¾ cups (660 ml) chicken broth

1 small carrot, peeled and diced (optional)

⅓ cup (50 g) green peas (if canned, drain, and if frozen, thaw) (optional)

1 sprig fresh cilantro (optional)

1 serrano pepper (optional)

Salt, to taste

1. Place the rice in a large heatproof bowl and add enough hot water to cover the rice. Stir once, then let stand for 15 minutes. Drain the rice in a strainer, then rinse it under cold water until the water runs clear. Shake the strainer well to remove any excess water, as the rice needs to be as dry as possible. Set aside to continue drying.

2. Heat the oil in a large saucepan or cazuela over medium-high heat, then add the rice. It should sizzle as it touches the oil. Fry until it starts to acquire a light golden-brown color, 8 to 10 minutes. Stir occasionally to ensure that the rice does not stick to the bottom of the pan. When it's done, carefully tip the pan to one side and use a spoon to remove the excess oil.

3. While the rice is cooking, place the tomatoes, onion, and garlic into a blender, and blend until smooth. Pour the tomato mixture into the rice using a strainer and stir. Continue cooking over medium-high heat until all the liquid has been absorbed, stirring to make sure the rice doesn't stick to the bottom of the pan, about 3 minutes. Stir in the chicken broth, any of the optional vegetables, and the salt, and bring to a boil.

4. Once it comes to a boil, cover the pan and cook over low heat until all the liquid has been absorbed and the rice and vegetables are cooked, about 15 minutes. Once you cover the rice, it is important not to stir or touch it until it is cooked; otherwise, it will become mushy. Check the rice to see if there is any moisture remaining (you might have to use a fork to check the bottom of the rice). If there is still some moisture, continue cooking over low heat for a few more minutes, still covered, until tender. Once the rice is cooked, remove from the heat and let stand, covered, for 10 to 15 minutes to let the rice continue steaming. Using a fork, lightly fluff the rice before serving.

NOTAS

✳ *Long-grain rice works best, as it renders a fluffy and moist end result. It has less starch content, so the grains of the cooked rice will not stick together, provided you rinse them well before cooking.*

✳ *Some people only rinse the rice. However, I've found that when you soak it, the grains are more tender and fluffier.*

ARROZ VERDE

Green Rice

This green rice is sometimes called *arroz poblano* because of the use of poblano peppers in the recipe. As with many recipes, each cook can add their personal touch, and some like to add epazote or parsley. Just like Arroz Rojo (page 132) and Arroz Blanco (page 130), this rice is delicious paired with many Mexican dishes.

PREP TIME: 15 minutes	**COOK TIME:** 35 minutes	**YIELD:** 6 servings

1 cup (270 g) long-grain white rice

1 large poblano pepper, roasted, seeded, and veins removed (see page 16 for roasting instructions)

1 romaine lettuce leaf

2 sprigs fresh cilantro, chopped

2 tablespoons (16 g) chopped white onion

1 clove garlic

2 cups (480 ml) chicken broth, divided

2 tablespoons (30 ml) vegetable oil

Salt, to taste

1. Place the rice in a large heatproof bowl and add enough hot water to cover the rice. Stir once, then let stand for 15 minutes. Drain the rice in a strainer, then rinse it under cold water until the water runs clear. Shake the strainer well to remove any excess water, as the rice needs to be as dry as possible. Set aside to continue drying.

2. Meanwhile, chop the roasted poblano pepper and place it in a blender, along with the lettuce leaf, cilantro, onion, and garlic. Add 1 cup (240 ml) of the chicken broth and blend until smooth. If it's not smooth, you will need to use a strainer to pour it over the rice in step 4. Set aside.

3. Heat the oil in a large saucepan over high heat. Once hot, add the rice and fry it, stirring frequently, until it has a light golden color, 6 to 7 minutes. Once it's done, carefully tip the pan to one side and remove the excess oil using a spoon.

4. Gently pour the poblano sauce into the pan, without stirring too much. Let it cook for about 3 minutes over medium-high heat, then add the remaining 1 cup (240 ml) chicken broth and season it with the salt. Once it comes to a boil, reduce the heat to low, cover, and cook for 12 to 15 minutes. Once you cover the rice, it is important not to stir until it is cooked; otherwise, it will become mushy.

5. By this time, the liquid will have been absorbed, and steam holes will have formed over the surface of the rice. Once the rice is cooked, remove from the heat and let stand, covered, for 10 to 15 minutes to let the rice continue steaming. Using a fork, lightly fluff the rice before serving, which will mix in any of the sauce that is at the bottom of the pan.

NOTAS

* Long-grain rice works best, as it renders a fluffy and moist end result. It has less starch content, so the grains of the cooked rice will not stick together, provided you rinse them well before cooking.

* Some people only rinse the rice. I've found that when you soak it, the grains are more tender and fluffier.

* For a greener color, use 2 medium poblano peppers instead of 1 large pepper.

* You can add corn kernels and strips of roasted poblano pepper to your rice with the chicken broth in step 4 or as a garnish at serving time.

* You can also serve the rice with a dollop of Mexican crema or sour cream.

FRIJOLES REFRITOS

Refried Beans

In Mexico, there are two ways of making fried beans: The first way is to lightly fry them in a pan with chopped onions and a small amount of fat (either lard or vegetable oil). The second way is what is called refried beans, which have a creamy and much smoother texture, and use a little bit more fat in the cooking process. I like to think of refried beans as more of a Sunday treat for breakfast or brunch. They are a perfect side dish for enchiladas, chilaquiles, fried eggs, and even tamales.

PREP TIME: 5 minutes	**COOK TIME:** 15 minutes	**YIELD:** 6 servings

3 tablespoons lard (45 g) or vegetable oil (45 ml)

⅓ cup (40 g) finely chopped white onion

3 cups (24 ounces/680 g) cooked or canned pinto or black beans, with about ½ cup (120 ml) of the cooking broth or liquid from the can

Salt, to taste

FOR GARNISHING

Queso fresco or other crumbling cheese

Tortilla chips

1. Heat the lard in a large skillet over medium-low heat. Add the onion and cook until they are transparent and start to turn brown, 4 to 5 minutes.

2. Add the beans to the pan with their broth and mash them using a bean or potato masher until they become a paste. Using a spatula, scrape the beans from the edges of the pan toward the center; this will help the beans cook thoroughly and they will begin to turn into a thick and creamy paste. Season with the salt.

3. Shake the skillet back and forth to form a roll with the bean paste. I like to flip it a bit like a pancake to form the roll. Taste to check if it needs more salt.

4. To serve, place the beans on a plate, sprinkle with the cheese, and garnish with some tortilla chips.

NOTAS

✶ *You can chop up some bacon or chorizo to include in the beans. Cook it in the pan before you add the onion in step 1. The amount of lard you add to the pan to cook the onions will depend on the amount of fat the meat renders.*

✶ *If you prefer your beans to be a little bit less dry, add more of the cooking broth from the beans.*

✶ *In place of the lard or vegetable oil, you can also use bacon or chorizo drippings; this will add a delicious flavor to the beans.*

FRIJOLES DE LA OLLA

Beans from the Pot

One of the simplest dishes you can enjoy in Mexican culture is a warm bowl of beans, preferably topped with some queso fresco and accompanied with a spicy salsa and some warm corn tortillas. As the name implies, these beans are traditionally cooked in a large clay pot, called *olla de barro*, which is believed to give the beans a special flavor when cooked over an open fire. Sadly, the romantic image of beans boiling in a clay pot over a wood fire is hardly attainable in today's modern and hectic world. Black beans are common fare in the Gulf Coast states of Veracruz, Campeche, Tabasco, and Yucatán, as well as in other parts of Mexico. Besides being served in their own broth as a stand-alone meal, black beans are commonly served as a side dish with only a little bit of their broth.

PREP TIME: 15 minutes	**COOK TIME:** 1 hour 30 minutes	**YIELD:** 8 servings

1 pound (450 g) dried black beans (about 2 heaping cups)

¼ large white onion

2 cloves garlic

8 cups (2 quarts/1.9 L) water

2 epazote leaves

1 serrano pepper (see Notas) (optional)

Salt, to taste

1 teaspoon lard or olive oil (optional)

1. First, you need to clean the beans. Place them on a large plate (or other flat surface) and use your fingers to move aside any broken or dried-up beans, as well as any small stones or other foreign material you find.

2. Thoroughly rinse the beans, then place them into a large stockpot with the onion, garlic, and water. Remove any beans that float to the surface, as these are probably too old and damaged. The beans will expand while cooking, which is why you need to use a large pot.

3. Cover the pot, turn the heat to medium high, and bring to a boil. Reduce the heat to simmer gently. The cooking time will depend on the freshness, size, and type of the beans, ranging from 1½ to 3 hours. Add hot water if needed during the cooking process in order to keep the water level 2 inches (5 cm) above the beans. Occasionally stir the beans.

4. When the beans are tender, add the epazote and serrano pepper (if using). Continue cooking until the beans are soft, then season with the salt and stir in the lard (if using) until incorporated.

NOTAS

* You can also make this recipe using pinto beans, just exclude the epazote.

* If using an Instant Pot, follow steps 1 and 2 of this recipe, then add the beans, onion, and garlic to the Instant Pot, along with 7 cups (1.7 L) water. Cook for 30 minutes on the Bean setting (with the valve closed), then open the valve and release the steam. Season with salt, add the lard or oil (if using), and cook for 5 more minutes on the Manual setting.

* If you use the serrano pepper, make a small slit in the center of the pepper with the tip of a sharp knife to allow the steam inside to escape and prevent the pepper from bursting during the cooking process.

* Do not add salt before cooking the beans, as the skins of the beans will turn tough, preventing them from becoming tender and causing them to burst.

* As a final step, some cooks like to mash a small amount of the cooked beans and then return them to the pot in order to have a thicker broth.

* Once the beans have cooled, they can be refrigerated for up to 4 days or frozen for up to 3 months.

FRIJOLES PINTOS CREMOSOS

Creamy Pinto Beans

With a creamy texture and light flavor, these pinto beans are the perfect side dish for a variety of meals. You can pair them with stews like Asado de Puerco (page 66) and Carne con Papas (page 65), or simply serve them alongside scrambled or fried eggs for breakfast. They are also an excellent filling for burritos. In Mexico, there is a large variety of beans available, some of which are only grown in certain regions and are unknown in other parts of the country. Even though I lived in the central and northern states of Mexico, where people tend to favor pinto beans, I am more accustomed to using black beans, since that's what my family used when I was growing up.

PREP TIME: 5 minutes	**COOK TIME:** 15 minutes	**YIELD:** 6 servings

2 tablespoons vegetable oil (30 ml) or lard (30 g)

¼ cup (30 g) finely chopped white onion

2½ cups (20 ounces/570 g) cooked or canned pinto beans, including their cooking broth or liquid from the can

Salt, to taste

FOR GARNISHING

Queso fresco or other crumbling cheese

Thinly sliced serrano peppers (optional)

1. Heat the oil in a large skillet over medium heat. Add the onion and cook until the edges turn brown, about 5 minutes.

2. Add the beans to the skillet, reserving the broth to add later. Using a bean or potato masher, mash the beans by pressing down on them until they have a pasty texture. If you don't have a masher, you can use the bottom of a heavy glass.

3. Add the bean broth, little by little. Stir and keep mashing the beans until they are creamy. Add more bean broth as needed to give the beans the desired consistency. Take off the heat and season with the salt.

4. Serve the beans topped with the cheese and serrano pepper slices (if using).

NOTAS

* *Make sure the beans you are using have been cooked until tender, to have a creamy texture when making this recipe.*

* *Once the beans have cooled down, they can be refrigerated for up to 2 days or frozen for up to a month.*

CALABACITAS CON CREMA

Mexican Squash with Cream

Calabacitas (squash) have been a part of the Mexican gastronomy since pre-Hispanic times, and ever since then, it has been planted alongside corn, beans, and peppers. Mexicans love to use squash in a variety of ways, like in stews and soups, as well as steamed, stuffed, or with salsa. Serve this as a side dish for grilled meats, chicken, fish, and milanesas, or as a filling for corn tortilla tacos and enchiladas and as a topping for tostadas.

PREP TIME: 15 minutes	**COOK TIME:** 20 minutes	**YIELD:** 6 servings

2 large poblano peppers

2 tablespoons (30 ml) vegetable or olive oil

½ white onion, chopped

2 cloves garlic, minced

1 pound (450 g) Mexican squash or zucchini, cut into ½-inch (1 cm) pieces

1 ear corn, with kernels removed, or ¾ cup (100 g) canned corn, drained, or frozen corn, thawed

Salt and pepper, to taste

1 teaspoon dried Mexican oregano

1 cup (230 g) Mexican crema or sour cream

½ cup (60 g) crumbled queso fresco, for garnishing (optional)

1. Roast the poblano peppers over an open flame of your stove over medium-high heat, turning for even roasting, 8 to 10 minutes. Place the roasted peppers in a plastic bag and close it, letting them steam for 5 minutes. Remove from the bag and scrape off the charred skin by rubbing your fingers on the surface of the peppers. Using a sharp knife, cut a slit along the length of the peppers and remove the seeds and veins. Cut the peppers into strips.

2. Heat the oil in a large skillet over medium-high heat. Add the onion and cook for 1 minute, then stir in the garlic and quickly cook until it releases its fragrance, less than a minute.

3. Add the squash and cook for 5 to 6 minutes, stirring occasionally, ensuring that it doesn't stick to the pan. Stir in the corn, cook for 1 more minute, then add the roasted poblano pepper strips. Season with the salt and pepper, and add the oregano (crumbled between your fingers).

4. Pour in the Mexican crema, stirring to make sure it coats all of the vegetables, and gently simmer for about 2 minutes. It will start to thicken by this time, and all the vegetables will be cooked.

5. Serve garnished with the queso fresco (if using).

NOTA *Squash and zucchini both cook quickly, so remove them from the heat while they're still undercooked and let them finish cooking in the heat of the sauce.*

CALABACITAS CON QUESO

Mexican Squash with Cheese

This dish can be used as a side dish and as a main course for those days when you want to have a meatless meal, by using this as a filling for tacos made with warm corn tortillas. Mexican squash has a slightly sweeter flavor compared to zucchini, and is delicious paired with cheese or cream, or just served by themselves, steamed and topped with a dab of butter.

PREP TIME: 10 minutes	**COOK TIME:** 20 minutes	**YIELD:** 4 servings

11 ounces (310 g) plum tomatoes (about 3 tomatoes), chopped

1 small clove garlic, chopped

¼ cup (60 ml) water

1 tablespoon (15 ml) vegetable or olive oil

1 tablespoon (15 g) butter

¼ cup (30 g) chopped white onion

2 sprigs fresh cilantro (optional)

13 ounces (370 g) Mexican squash (about 2 medium squash) or zucchini, diced

Salt, to taste

7 ounces (200 g) panela cheese, cut into ⅔-inch (1.5 cm) cubes

1. Place the tomatoes and garlic in a blender with the water, and blend until smooth. Set aside.

2. In a medium skillet, heat the oil and butter over medium-high heat. Add the onion and cook until transparent, 2 to 3 minutes.

3. Add the tomato sauce and cilantro (if using) to the pan, and cook for 3 more minutes. Stir in the squash and season with the salt. Cook for 10 to 12 more minutes until the squash is tender and the tomato sauce is cooked. Just before serving, stir in the cheese.

NOTAS

✱ *If you like spicy food, add 1 serrano pepper or ½ jalapeño pepper to the sauce when you blend it in step 1.*

✱ *Queso fresco can be substituted for the panela cheese. If you can't find either of these cheeses, you can use feta, but remember that feta is a salty cheese, so take that into account when seasoning the tomato sauce.*

ENSALADA DE REPOLLO

Cabbage Salad

In Mexico, most vegetables are used as ingredients in stews, as in the case of squash, carrots, green beans, and chayotes; however, they are also used to make salads, especially simple ones, like this cabbage salad my mom used to make. I like to serve this with fried fish or grilled meats. One of the many uses for this cabbage salad is as a topping for tacos, either soft tacos or flautas.

PREP TIME: 15 minutes	**YIELD:** 4 servings

4 cups (240 g) shredded green cabbage

4 radishes, thinly sliced

½ white onion, sliced

2 tablespoons (30 ml) olive or vegetable oil

Juice of 1 lime

Salt and pepper, to taste

1 large tomato, sliced

1. Place the cabbage, radishes, and white onion in a large bowl or on a serving plate.

2. In a small bowl, combine the oil, lime juice, salt, and pepper for a vinaigrette. Mix well.

3. Pour the vinaigrette onto the cabbage and mix thoroughly. Let rest for about 6 to 8 minutes.

4. Just before serving, decorate the salad with the tomato slices.

NOTA *Not everyone likes the flavor of cabbage. If you want a milder flavor, choose a large cabbage. The smaller, brighter-colored cabbages have a stronger flavor.*

NOPALES CON OREGANO

Cactus Paddles with Oregano

I love using *nopales* when cooking Mexican dishes. Its texture is soft and the flavor is similar to that of okra. Cactus paddles are used in a variety of ways in Mexican dishes—in soups and stews, scrambled with eggs, or grilled and topped with melted cheese. Additionally, they are rich in fiber, vitamins, and other nutrients. If you have never eaten nopales, I hope you give them a try with this easy recipe, which can also be used as a filling for tacos, topped with crumbled Mexican cheese and a spicy salsa.

PREP TIME: 5 minutes	**COOK TIME:** 20 minutes	**YIELD:** 4 servings

8 ounces (225 g) nopales (about 2½ cups), cleaned and diced (see page 9 for nopales prep)

1 tablespoon (15 ml) olive oil

4 teaspoons diced white onion

1 teaspoon dried Mexican oregano

Salt and pepper, to taste

1. To precook the nopales, place the nopales in a small saucepan and cover them with water. Turn the heat to high and bring to a boil, then reduce the heat and simmer for 8 minutes. Drain and set aside.

2. Heat the oil in a skillet over medium-high heat. Add the chopped onion and cook for 5 minutes, until it becomes transparent.

3. Stir in the nopales, then season with the oregano, salt, and pepper, and continue cooking for 4 to 5 minutes.

NOTA *If you can't find fresh nopales, you can use nopales sold in a jar.*

DESSERTS
& DRINKS

ARROZ CON LECHE

Rice Pudding

One of the most popular desserts in Mexican cuisine is rice pudding. This dessert can be made very quickly, and uses ingredients you probably already have in your kitchen. This recipe brings back a lot of sweet childhood memories. When I make this recipe, I like to use condensed milk, as it gives an extra-creamy texture to the rice pudding.

PREP TIME: 5 minutes	**COOK TIME:** 30 minutes	**YIELD:** 6 servings

2½ cups (600 ml) water

¾ cup (140 g) short-grain white rice

2-inch (5 cm) Mexican cinnamon stick

¾ cup (180 ml) whole milk

½ cup (155 g) sweetened condensed milk

¼ cup (35 g) raisins (optional)

Ground cinnamon, for dusting

NOTAS

✱ *Short-grain rice has a higher starch content, which will render a creamier rice pudding.*

✱ *You can use skim or 2% milk instead of whole milk. You will have to add a little more milk during the final cooking stage in step 4 if you want to achieve the same creamy consistency you would get with whole milk.*

✱ *The sweetness of the condensed milk will be enough for many, but if you have a sweeter tooth, drizzle some more on the rice pudding when serving.*

✱ *Other good flavorings for this pudding include vanilla, lemon, or orange rind, or even the leaves of orange trees.*

1. Place the water, rice, and cinnamon stick in a medium saucepan over high heat. Bring to a boil, then reduce the heat to a simmer and cook, uncovered, until the rice is tender, about 20 minutes. The rice is ready when all the water has evaporated and it has formed some holes on the surface.

2. While the rice is cooking, combine the whole milk with the condensed milk in a medium bowl and stir well.

3. Remove the saucepan from the heat. Pour the milk mixture into the saucepan and stir. If you would like to add raisins, add them now.

4. Return the saucepan to the heat and continue cooking over medium heat until the pudding thickens, 5 to 10 minutes, stirring occasionally to keep it from sticking to the bottom of the saucepan. If the rice looks too dry for your taste, add an extra ¼ cup (60 ml) warm whole milk and stir. The end result should be a soft and creamy pudding.

5. If serving warm, place the pudding in small bowls and sprinkle with the ground cinnamon. If you want to serve the pudding cold, pour it into a container and cover with plastic wrap, pressed down onto the rice's surface to prevent a skin from forming, and refrigerate for up to 3 days. Dust it with cinnamon before serving.

BUDÍN DE PAN

Bread Pudding

Budín de pan can be found in almost every bakery in Mexico. Bakers make this using bread that went unsold the day before. Some bakers add extra ingredients to enhance the pudding, like shredded coconut, candied figs, and chopped pecans, in addition to the popular use of raisins. This pudding can be made with leftover toast, a sweet roll that has become stale, a piece of French bread, and so on (see Notas). I like to collect all the bits and pieces of leftover bread and store them in the freezer in a gallon-size (3.8 L) freezer bag. When it's full, it means it's time to make this recipe. Enjoy this bread pudding with a cup of coffee.

PREP TIME: 25 minutes	**COOK TIME:** 50 minutes	**YIELD:** 12 servings

⅓ cup (80 g) butter, melted and cooled, plus more for greasing

17½ ounces (500 g) day-old bread (see Notas), cut into pieces or cubes

3 cups (710 ml) whole milk

3 large eggs

½ cup (100 g) sugar

1 teaspoon vanilla extract

1 teaspoon ground cinnamon

½ cup (70 g) raisins

1½ Mexican cinnamon sticks (optional)

Honey or syrup of your choice, to serve

1. Preheat the oven to 350°F (175°C). Grease an 8 x 8-inch (20 cm) square baking dish with butter.

2. Place the bread cubes in a large bowl and pour the milk over them. Let them soak in the milk for 10 to 15 minutes so they can soften. Using your hands or a fork, break apart any large pieces of bread.

3. Beat the eggs in a small bowl and pour them into the bread mixture, then add the melted butter, sugar, vanilla extract, cinnamon, and raisins. Using a spatula, gently mix these ingredients together until you have a uniform mixture. Pour the mixture into the greased baking dish, smoothing out the surface with a spatula. Break the cinnamon sticks (if using), into pieces and insert them into different places in the pudding. A portion of each cinnamon piece should be sticking out of the surface; this will make it easier to pull them out before eating.

4. Bake for 50 to 60 minutes. To test if the pudding is done, insert a toothpick into the center to see if it comes out clean. The top surface of the pudding will form a crust, but the bread underneath will still feel soft. When you first take the pudding out of the oven, it will look fluffy, but this fluffiness will reduce as the bread cools. Wait for the pudding to cool a bit before cutting it.

5. Serve with the honey or syrup.

NOTAS

✖ You can use a mixture of different types of bread for this recipe. Some examples include sandwich bread, hot dog buns, sweetened breads, and French rolls. Keep in mind that the types of bread used will affect the amount of sugar needed, so check the sweetness of the bread mixture in step 2 to see if it needs more sugar for your taste.

✖ In addition to the raisins, you can also add ⅓ cup (25 g) of shredded coconut or ¼ cup (25 g) chopped pecans to the pudding mixture in step 3.

✖ The addition of the cinnamon sticks is optional; it's just something I like to do, as this is the way I remember seeing bread pudding being sold in my hometown when I was growing up. The cinnamon pieces will add more flavor to the bread, and your kitchen will smell wonderful while you're baking it.

BUÑUELOS

Buñuelos are a sweet treat that has a special place in the hearts of many. I am sure a lot of Mexicans living abroad remember making buñuelos with their mothers, grandmothers, and aunts during Christmastime. Making these with the younger generations is an excellent way of creating memories and keeping traditions alive.

PREP TIME: 50 minutes	**COOK TIME:** 20 minutes	**YIELD:** 12

PILONCILLO SYRUP

3½ cups (840 ml) water, divided

1 large piloncillo cone (about 12 ounces/340 g)

1 Mexican cinnamon stick

6 guavas, chopped or cut into quarters

⅓ teaspoon anise seeds

¼ of an orange peel

BUÑUELOS

2 cups (260 g) all-purpose flour, plus more for dusting your work space

1 teaspoon baking powder

1 tablespoon (13 g) sugar

½ teaspoon salt

1 egg

1 tablespoon (15 g) butter, melted and cooled

1 teaspoon vanilla extract

About ¾ cup (180 ml) warm water

Vegetable oil, for frying

Sugar, for sprinkling

1. To make the piloncillo syrup: Place 1 cup (240 ml) of the water and the piloncillo in a medium saucepan over medium-high heat. Heat until the piloncillo dissolves and looks like liquid caramel. Carefully add the remaining 2½ cups (600 ml) water to the pan, along with the cinnamon stick, guavas, anise seeds, and orange peel. Bring to a boil over medium-high heat, then reduce the heat and simmer for 10 minutes. Strain the syrup into a small bowl or other container. Set aside to drizzle as a topping. You can serve it warm or at room temperature.

2. To make the buñuelos: In a large bowl, combine the flour, baking powder, sugar, and salt. Form a well in the center and add the egg, melted butter, and vanilla extract. Mix the ingredients together until the mixture resembles coarse meal. Slowly add the warm water, a tablespoon (15 ml) at a time, mixing and kneading until you have a soft and smooth dough; this will take less than 5 minutes. Cover the dough with a cloth kitchen towel and let rest for 30 minutes.

3. Divide the dough into 12 small balls and cover them with a kitchen towel. Add the oil to a large skillet so that it is ¾ inch (2 cm) deep and heat over medium-high heat to about 350°F (175°C). Place a dough ball on a floured work surface and roll it out with a rolling pin to form a circle as thin as possible without breaking the dough. The buñuelos should be thin and almost transparent. To stretch them even more, you can place the rolled-out dough on an inverted bowl (covered in a pastry cloth) and pull gently on the edges (this step is entirely optional). Repeat this process for the remaining dough balls.

4. Fry the buñuelos, one at a time, in the hot oil for 20 to 30 seconds on each side, flipping once, until they are golden and crispy. Place the fried buñuelos on a paper towel–lined plate to drain the excess oil.

5. Serve warm or at room temperature with the piloncillo syrup. Don't sprinkle with the sugar until serving them.

NOTAS

✖ *This recipe is easy to prepare, and you can make more than one batch to store and then reheat in the oven at 250°F (120°C) for 5 minutes.*

✖ *If you want your piloncillo syrup thicker, simmer it for a longer period of time. The syrup will keep in the refrigerator for up to 1 week.*

✖ *You can substitute the water and vanilla extract in the dough with anise tea. To make anise tea, bring 1½ cups (360 ml) water to a boil, then add ½ teaspoon anise seeds and set aside to cool. Strain the tea and use the amount needed to make the dough. Another substitute for the vanilla extract is orange liqueur or orange extract.*

✖ *After forming the buñuelos, some people lay them out on a large table covered with a clean tablecloth, ensuring they're not touching each other. This will dry the dough, making the buñuelos even crispier, and they will absorb less oil while cooking.*

✖ *If you do not sprinkle the finished buñuelos with sugar immediately after frying, they will remain nice and crispy for up to 2 more days; simply add the sugar at serving time.*

CHURROS

Growing up, a trip to downtown Tampico meant an obligatory stop at a restaurant called El Elite. Just two blocks from the cathedral, and across the street from Sears, this restaurant had a street stand right in front where passersby could buy aguas frescas and the restaurant's most popular item: churros. This place is still an icon in my hometown, and the locals know that you will always find some of the best churros there. Please read all the notes and instructions in this recipe before you start for the best results.

PREP TIME: 10 minutes	**COOK TIME:** 20 minutes	**YIELD:** 12 churros

2½ cups (600 ml) vegetable or canola oil, for frying

1 cup (240 ml) water

1 teaspoon vanilla extract

⅛ teaspoon salt

2 tablespoons (30 g) butter

1 cup (130 g) all-purpose flour, sifted at least 2 times

1 large egg, beaten

½ cup (100 g) sugar

1 teaspoon ground cinnamon (optional)

NOTAS

* *Keeping an eye on the temperature of the oil at 350°F (175°C) is very important for this recipe.*

* *You can also pipe the strips of dough directly into the hot oil, cutting them with kitchen scissors to form the churros. The oil will start bubbling when you add the raw churros. At this point it is important not to touch the churro or the oil right away, as it might cause the churro to explode.*

1. Heat the oil in a large skillet to 350°F (175°C) while you make the churro batter. You can use a candy or laser thermometer to check the temperature of the oil.

2. Place the water, vanilla extract, salt, and butter in a medium saucepan over medium-high heat. Bring to a rolling boil, then stir in the flour all at once. It is very important that the water is boiling when you add the flour, in order to ensure that the dough will render crispy churros. Vigorously mix the dough using a wooden spoon or spatula (you need to do this very quickly).

3. Remove the saucepan from the heat, wait about 1 minute, and then add the egg. Keep mixing until the egg is completely integrated into the dough (use a stand mixer for this step). In the beginning, the dough will want to separate after adding the egg, but keep mixing until the ingredients are well combined and you have a smooth and soft dough that comes away from the bottom of the pot. This will take a few minutes.

4. Place the dough in a pastry bag fitted with a star-shaped tip. Make sure there aren't any air bubbles in the dough. Line a tray with parchment paper, then pipe 6-inch (15 cm) strips of dough onto the prepared tray.

5. Fry the churros, 4 to 6 at a time, for about 2 to 2½ minutes in the hot oil until golden brown, then turn them over and continue frying for an even crispiness and golden color, for a total of 4 to 5 minutes. Once the churros are golden, remove them from the hot oil and place them on a paper towel–lined tray to drain the excess oil.

6. Place the sugar (mixed with the cinnamon, if using) in a shallow dish and dredge the churros before serving.

CREPAS

Crepes

In Mexico, crepes are made with both sweet and savory fillings, but sweet crepes are more common. One of the most popular sweet fillings is *cajeta*, which is similar to dulce de leche but made using goat's milk. I have lived twice in the city of Toluca, near Mexico City, and while living there, I learned about the locals' liking for crepes, especially at parties and other social gatherings. I usually make crepes when we want a quick dessert that doesn't require any baking. In my home, we stuff them with strawberries and cream for a perfect after-dinner treat.

PREP TIME: 10 minutes	**COOK TIME:** 20 minutes	**YIELD:** 12 crepes

¾ cup (100 g) all-purpose flour

2 eggs

1¼ cups (300 ml) whole milk

½ teaspoon sugar

Pinch salt

¼ cup (60 ml) vegetable oil or melted butter, plus more oil or butter for greasing

NOTA *Crepes can be refrigerated for up to 6 days. Reheat them, one at a time, in a skillet over low heat for about 30 seconds per side.*

1. Add the flour, eggs, milk, sugar, and salt to a large bowl. Mix together, then add the oil. Mix together the ingredients until the batter has a uniform texture. Set aside.

2. Heat a medium nonstick skillet over medium-high heat. Grease the pan with a small dab of oil or butter (you can use a pastry brush or a paper towel to apply it). Line a plate with paper towels.

3. Pour ¼ cup (60 ml) of the batter into the pan. Tilt the pan around to make sure that the batter completely coats the entire flat surface. Cook until the edges of the crepe look a little bit dry and start to curl up, 1 to 2 minutes. Flip the crepe over and cook for about 10 seconds, or until you see brown spots forming on the bottom side of the crepe. Remove the crepe and place it the prepared plate. Repeat this process with the remaining batter.

4. To serve, fill the crepes with a sweet or savory filling and fold in half or in quarters (you can also roll them up like a taco).

FLAN

This easy recipe for Mexican-style flan has been well-known in Mexico for years. It is made using whole eggs, condensed milk, and evaporated milk, and covered with a light caramel syrup. You can also make this flan using cream cheese or coconut milk for a different taste and texture. This is not the traditional, old-fashioned way of making flan, as it is usually prepared as a custard where the milk, vanilla, and sugar are slowly simmered.

PREP TIME: 15 minutes	COOK TIME: 50 minutes	YIELD: 12 servings

1 cup (200 g) sugar

2 tablespoons (30 ml) water

1 can (14 ounces/397 ml) condensed milk

1 can (12 ounces/354 ml) evaporated milk

6 large eggs

1 teaspoon vanilla extract

NOTAS

✳ *If you want your flan to have an even creamier texture, add one 8-ounce (225 g) package of cream cheese to the blender when you are preparing the milk and egg mixture in step 3.*

✳ *Store any leftovers in the refrigerator for up to 4 days.*

1. Place the sugar and water in a medium saucepan over high heat. Bring to a boil until the sugar dissolves. Reduce the heat and keep boiling until the syrup is a light-brown caramel color, about 10 minutes.

2. Pour the caramel into an 8-inch (20 cm) round baking pan, swirling it around so that the caramel evenly coats the bottom. Let cool completely. Preheat the oven to 325°F (160°C).

3. Add the condensed and evaporated milks, eggs, and vanilla extract to a blender, and blend until a smooth mixture. Slowly pour this mixture into the pan with the cooled caramel and cover with aluminum foil.

4. For the water bath (bain-marie), place this pan inside a larger baking pan. Add warm water to the larger pan until it is ¾ inch (2 cm) deep.

5. Bake for about 50 minutes, or until the flan looks firm. It will keep cooking while it cools, so do not let it stay in the oven any longer. Allow it to cool in the pan for at least 6 hours before serving.

6. Once the flan has cooled, run a knife between the flan and the sides of the baking pan. Place a large serving plate on top of the pan and quickly invert it to avoid spilling any liquid caramel from the container. Slide the pan off the flan and serve.

GELATINA DE MOSAICO

Mosaic Gelatin

Mexicans love gelatins of all shapes and sizes. You can find colorful gelatins sold at markets, state fairs, central plazas, and food carts. They can be prepared using a water or milk base, and can have a single flavor or multiple ones. Some people make them with intricate designs, ranging from flowers and hearts to butterflies. This is a colorful gelatin that is perfectly at home at a child's birthday party, and is loved by kids and adults alike.

PREP TIME: 30 minutes plus 8 hours chilling time	**COOK TIME:** 10 minutes	**YIELD:** 16 servings

1 box (3 ounces/85 g) cherry gelatin

1 box (3 ounces/85 g) strawberry gelatin

1 box (3 ounces/85 g) orange gelatin

1 box (3 ounces/85 g) lime gelatin

4 cups (1 quart/950 ml) water

1 tablespoon (15 ml) vegetable oil

¾ cup (180 ml) cold water

4 packages (¼ ounce/7 grams each) unflavored gelatin

1 can (14 ounces/397 ml) condensed milk

1 can (12 ounces/354 ml) evaporated milk

1 can (7.6 ounces/225 g) media crema table cream or 1 cup (240 ml) heavy whipping cream

2 teaspoons vanilla extract

1. Pour each of the 4 gelatin flavors into a separate heatproof container. Bring the water to a boil in a large saucepan, then pour 1 cup (240 ml) of boiling water into each container. Stir each gelatin well, making sure that all the granules have dissolved. Set the containers aside to cool, then refrigerate for 2 hours. If you wish, you can do this step a day ahead of assembling this dessert.

2. Grease the inside of a 7 x 11-inch (18 x 28 cm) rectangular pan or large Bundt cake mold with the vegetable oil to help the gelatin be removed easily. Remove the 4 flavored gelatins from the refrigerator and cut them into ⅜- or ½-inch (1 or 1.3 cm) cubes. Do not cut them any smaller. Place about one-quarter of the flavored gelatin cubes at the bottom of the greased pan. Mix the colors to give the gelatin a beautiful, colorful appearance.

3. Pour the cold water into a medium heatproof bowl, then add the unflavored gelatin. Mix well to dissolve any lumps. Let rest for 5 minutes to allow the gelatin to bloom. Place this bowl in the microwave and heat for 45 seconds until the gelatin dissolves and is completely liquid. You can also warm the bowl in a bain-marie for about 5 minutes. Let the mixture cool completely.

4. Pour the condensed and evaporated milks and the table cream into a blender, along with the vanilla extract. Blend on high for 30 seconds, then add the unflavored gelatin liquid, little by little. Turn off the blender when all the ingredients in the mixture are well combined. Pour this mixture into the pan with the flavored gelatin, then add the remainder of the flavored gelatin cubes, mixing the colors. Refrigerate for 8 hours, or overnight.

5. To serve, remove the gelatin from the refrigerator and allow it to come to room temperature. Run a knife around the edges of the pan, then place a plate on top of the pan and quickly invert it to remove the gelatin. Cut into squares.

NOTAS

* *The unflavored gelatin needs to be completely cooled in step 4, because if it is still warm, it will curdle the milks and spoil the whole mixture.*

* *It is best to refrigerate the gelatin for 8 hours, or overnight, this way it will be firmer and easier to cut and remove from the pan at serving time. If you are in a hurry, the minimum time you should refrigerate it is 6 hours.*

* *If you don't want to invert the pan to remove the gelatin, you can cut and serve the gelatin from the pan.*

PASTEL DE CUMPLEAÑOS

Old-Fashioned Birthday Cake

This recipe is for a cake that my family knows simply as *pastel de cumpleaños*, since I only make it for birthdays. Of course, this doesn't mean that it can't be made on other occasions, but for my family, this is a special treat. My neighbor Tey gave me this recipe when I was living in central Mexico in the early 1980s. I remember she was having a party at her house to celebrate her daughter's birthday, and as I was grabbing a second serving of the cake, I thought to myself, I need to know how to make this. Growing up, I liked birthday cakes decorated with meringue; they have an old-fashioned taste that you can't find these days.

PREP TIME: 40 minutes	**COOK TIME:** 45 minutes	**YIELD:** 12 servings

CAKES

2 sticks (240 g) unsalted butter, at room temperature, plus more for preparing the pans

3 cups (390 g) all-purpose flour, sifted, plus more for preparing the pans

3 teaspoons baking powder

½ teaspoon salt

1½ cups (300 g) sugar

4 large eggs, at room temperature

Zest of 1 orange

1 cup (240 ml) fresh orange juice

1½ cups (435 g) strawberry preserves or orange marmalade

MERINGUE TOPPING

1¼ cups (250 g) sugar

¼ cup (60 ml) water

4 large egg whites

1 teaspoon vanilla extract

½ teaspoon fresh lime juice or ¼ teaspoon cream of tartar

1. To make the cakes: Preheat the oven to 350°F (175°C). Butter and flour two 9 x 2-inch deep (23 x 5 cm) layer cake pans, tapping out any excess flour.

2. Place the flour, baking powder, and salt in a medium bowl and whisk together. Set aside.

3. In a large bowl, using a hand mixer (or a stand mixer fitted with the whisk attachment), beat the butter and sugar until the mixture is light and creamy, about 3 minutes. Use a rubber spatula to scrape the sides of the bowl to make sure the butter and sugar are well combined. Add the eggs, one at a time, beating at high speed, then mix in the orange zest, about 2 minutes. Reduce the speed to low and add the dry ingredients and the orange juice to the bowl, alternating the ingredients, adding a bit of the flour mixture followed by a bit of the orange juice, and repeating until all the ingredients are combined. You may need to use your spatula to make sure the batter is well mixed and there are no clumps of flour at the bottom of the bowl. Divide the batter between the prepared pans.

4. Bake for 28 to 30 minutes, or until a toothpick inserted into the cakes' centers comes out clean. Remove from the oven and let completely cool before removing from the pans. Set aside.

(continued)

5. To make the meringue topping: Place the sugar and water in a small saucepan over medium-high heat. Simmer to dissolve the sugar, swirling the pan around to make sure all the sugar gets dissolved. Once the sugar is liquid, remove from the heat and set aside.

6. Place the egg whites in a large bowl and beat at high speed, using a stand or handheld mixer, until they start turning foamy. Add the vanilla extract and lime juice. Continue beating at high speed and slowly add the hot sugar syrup, gently pouring the syrup into one side of the bowl. The meringue is ready once it forms soft and glossy peaks that hold their shape. This takes 6 to 7 minutes, and the meringue should still feel warm.

7. Once the cakes have cooled, it's time to assemble them. Make sure the tops of both cakes are level, as they are going to be layered on each other. If not level, slice off the tops with a serrated knife.

8. Place one cake on a large round cake plate or serving plate. Warm the strawberry preserves in the microwave or a bain-marie, just enough for it to be spreadable. Spread the warmed preserves evenly over the top of this cake. Place the second cake/layer on top of this cake.

9. To decorate, add one-quarter of the meringue on top of the cake and spread it toward the side of the cake with a spatula. Keep adding more meringue in stages until the entire cake is covered. Wait at least 1 hour before serving the cake to allow the meringue and the preserves to cool down and help stabilize the cake; otherwise, the cake layers will separate when cutting.

10. Cut the cake into slices and serve on small plates.

NOTAS

* All ingredients in this recipe, for the cakes and the meringue topping, should be at room temperature.

* If you only have salted butter for making the cake, omit the ½ teaspoon salt.

* If you like a generous amount of meringue on your cake, add an extra egg white when making the meringue.

* The cake should be completely cool before decorating.

* Instead of the meringue, you can decorate the cake with a whipped-cream topping. Make it following the instructions in the Pastel de Tres Leches recipe (opposite).

PASTEL DE TRES LECHES

Three Milks Cake

Made in Mexico and other Latin-American countries, *pastel de tres leches* is a sponge cake soaked in a mixture of different milks and creams. It's called *tres leches* because it is made with condensed milk, evaporated milk, and canned cream. This recipe is a little different than other recipes for this cake, resulting in a cake with a denser texture than recipes that use an egg-heavy batter. This richer texture makes for a better mouthfeel. It will take a little longer for the cake to absorb the milk mixture, but trust me, the wait is worth it.

PREP TIME: 30 minutes plus 6 to 8 hours resting time	**COOK TIME:** 35 minutes	**YIELD:** 12 servings

CAKE

1 stick (120 g) unsalted butter, melted and cooled, plus more for preparing the pan

1¼ cups (165 g) all-purpose flour, sifted, plus more for preparing the pan

1 teaspoon baking powder

¼ teaspoon salt

5 large eggs

1 cup (200 g) sugar

1 teaspoon vanilla extract

MILK MIXTURE

1 can (14 ounces/397 ml) condensed milk

1 can (12 ounces/354 ml) evaporated milk

1 can (7.6 ounces/225 g) media crema table cream or 1 cup (240 g) heavy whipping cream

1½ teaspoons vanilla extract

WHIPPED-CREAM TOPPING

1¼ cups (300 ml) heavy whipping cream

¼ cup (45 g) superfine sugar

1 teaspoon vanilla extract

GARNISHING AND TO SERVE

Assorted fresh or canned fruit, like peaches, mangos, strawberries, kiwis, etc.

1. To make the cake: Preheat the oven to 325°F (160°C). Place the oven rack in the middle position. Butter and flour a 13 x 9-inch (33 x 23 cm) baking pan and set aside.

2. Place the flour, baking powder, and salt in a medium bowl and mix together.

3. Beat the eggs, one by one, in a large bowl using a hand mixer on medium speed. Beat for 45 to 60 seconds each. Once you've beaten all the eggs, slowly add the sugar until it's fully incorporated. The egg mixture will be very fluffy and turn a pale-yellow color.

4. Reduce the speed of the mixer to low, then slowly add the melted butter, little by little, followed by the vanilla extract. Turn off the mixer once all the ingredients are combined.

5. Add the flour mixture, spoonful by spoonful, and gently fold it into the egg mixture with a spatula. Mix until well combined, but don't overmix the batter. Pour the batter into the prepared pan, using a spatula to help evenly spread it.

6. Bake for 30 to 35 minutes, or until the cake looks light golden and a toothpick inserted into its center comes out clean. Remove from the oven and transfer to a wire rack to cool completely. Poke holes all over the top of the cake using a toothpick, skewer, or fork; these will help the cake absorb the milk mixture better.

(continued)

7. To make the milk mixture: Whisk together the condensed and evaporated milks and the table cream in a medium saucepan. Stir in the vanilla extract, then warm the ingredients over low heat until they're completely combined. Remove from the heat and set aside.

8. Once the cake has cooled, slowly drizzle the milk mixture over the cake. Cover the cake with plastic wrap and refrigerate for 6 to 8 hours, or overnight, for best results; this will allow the cake to thoroughly absorb the liquid.

9. To make the whipped-cream topping: Place the heavy cream, superfine sugar, and vanilla extract in a cold large bowl. Using a hand mixer on medium speed, mix the ingredients until soft peaks form, about 2 minutes.

10. To assemble the cake, spread the whipped-cream topping all over the cake with a spatula. Keep refrigerated until ready to serve.

11. Decorate with the assorted fruit just before slicing and serving.

NOTAS

* *If you want your cake to be a little taller, use a 7 x 11-inch (18 x 28 cm) rectangular pan or an 8 x 8-inch (20 x 20 cm) square pan.*

* *The butter must be melted and cooled, otherwise the egg mixture will deflate, resulting in a flat cake. If you only have salted butter for making the cake batter, then omit the ¼ teaspoon salt.*

* *Some people mix together the milks while cold and then proceed to pour the mixture over the cake. I feel that warming the milks helps them combine better and enhances the flavors of the cake.*

* *Some cooks like to add a little bit of rum or brandy to the cake. If you want to do this, add ¼ cup (60 ml) to the milk mixture when you add the vanilla extract in step 7.*

* *I place the mixer beaters in the freezer and the bowl in the refrigerator before making the whipping cream. This trick always helps to achieve a smooth and fluffy whipped cream.*

* *If you want to make the fruit on top of the cake look shiny, use a pastry brush to glaze them with a mixture of apricot preserves and water. To make the glaze, mix ¼ cup (60 ml) water and ¼ cup (75 g) apricot preserves in a small saucepan. Heat over low heat until a light syrup forms, about 5 minutes. Let cool completely before brushing on the fruit.*

TAMALES DULCES

Sweet Tamales

When making savory tamales, some families separate a small amount of the masa harina to make these sweet tamales, which we call *tamales sulces* or *tamales de dulce*. There's the simple version that only contains some sugar, but you can also add fillings, like raisins, pineapple chunks, and shredded coconut, just to name a few. Raisins are the most popular addition.

PREP TIME: 40 minutes	**COOK TIME:** 1 hour	**YIELD:** 10 tamales

10 large corn husks, plus 10 more for lining the steaming pot

1 stick (120 g) unsalted butter or lard, at room temperature

1½ cups (185 g) masa harina

¼ teaspoon baking powder

6 tablespoons (75 g) sugar

1½ cups (360 ml) warm water

6 drops red food coloring

2 tablespoons (18 g) raisins

1. Place all the corn husks in a large bowl and cover them with hot water to soften; this will help make the husks soft and easily pliable when preparing the tamales. Remove the husks, drain any excess water, and set aside.

2. Place the butter in a large bowl, then beat it with a hand or stand mixer for a couple minutes until it has a creamy texture, about 2 minutes. Continue beating the butter, then slowly add the masa harina, baking powder, and sugar. Mix well, then add the warm water, little by little, until the dough has a smooth texture. While mixing the ingredients, add the food coloring, mixing well for a uniform color. The dough should look slightly pink. Stir in the raisins. Unless using a stand mixer, beat the dough with your hands or a wooden spoon until it has a creamy texture. The dough will be too heavy to work with using a hand mixer. The dough is ready when it looks fluffy and creamy, like very soft ice cream. If your dough seems too dry, add a little more water. The consistency has to be very soft.

3. To assemble the tamales, place a corn husk on your work surface with the wide end facing toward you. Place about ⅓ cup (80 g) of the dough in the center of the corn husk, closer to the bottom of the husk (the wide end). Using the back of a large spoon, evenly spread the dough toward the left, right, and bottom edges. The dough should reach all the way to the bottom edge (or just before it) but leave an inch (2.5 cm) of space on the left and right sides. Fold the right and left sides of the corn husk in toward the center, overlapping each other and completely covering the dough and the filling. Next, fold the narrow end of the husk up toward the center. Repeat this process with the remaining 9 corn husks and dough. I usually line up the formed tamales on a tray as I make them.

4. To steam the tamales, place a steamer rack inside a large stockpot. Add enough warm water so that it almost reaches the steamer rack, then line the rack with a layer of corn husks. Place the tamales in the pot in an upright position, with the open ends facing up. Cover them with a generous layer of husks, then cover the pot. Steam the tamales for about 1 hour over medium heat. During the steaming, check the pot to see if it has enough water (be careful when removing the lid), adding more if needed (see Notas). To check if the tamales are ready, remove one from the pot, wait 5 minutes, then open it. If the husk separates easily from the dough when you open it, that means that the tamal is ready. If the dough sticks to the husk, place it back in the pot and cook for 15 more minutes.

5. Serve the tamales while still hot; just let them rest for 5 minutes so the dough can firm up.

NOTAS

* *You can always skip the artificial food coloring, or you can buy natural food coloring at specialty or organic stores.*

* *Taste the dough for sweetness. You may want to add some extra sugar if you have a sweeter tooth.*

* *If you need to add more water to the pot when steaming the tamales, make sure to pour it as close to the wall of the pot as possible, avoiding the tamales. If water gets into the tamales, they will lose their flavor and the dough will be soggy.*

* *You can store the tamales in plastic bags in your freezer for up to 4 months. To reheat them, allow them to defrost, then place them in a steamer for 10 to 15 minutes. You can also pop them in the microwave on a high setting for about 1 minute.*

TAMALES DE PIÑA
Pineapple Tamales

Tamales de piña are one of the most popular sweet tamales in Mexico, after Tamales Dulces (page 168). These tamales are often made with only pineapple in the dough, but for this recipe I added raisins, shredded coconut, and chopped pecans. They make an excellent dessert, served with a cup of coffee. If you like, you can top them with whipped cream or drizzle them with condensed milk.

PREP TIME: 35 minutes	**COOK TIME:** 45 minutes	**YIELD:** 12 small tamales

12 small corn husks, plus 10 more for lining the steaming pot

1 stick (120 g) butter, at room temperature

2 cups (245 g) masa harina

6 tablespoons (75 g) sugar

½ teaspoon baking powder

¾ cup (180 ml) pineapple juice (from the can of pineapples) or water

1 teaspoon vanilla extract

⅔ cup (130 g) diced canned pineapple

¼ cup (35 g) raisins

¼ cup (18 g) unsweetened shredded coconut

¼ cup (25 g) chopped pecans

1. Place all the corn husks in a large bowl and cover them with hot water to soften; this will help make the husks soft and easily pliable when preparing the tamales. Remove the husks, drain any excess water, and set aside.

2. Place the butter in a large bowl, then beat it with a hand mixer or spatula for a couple minutes, until it has a creamy texture. Gradually add the masa harina, sugar, baking powder, pineapple juice, and vanilla extract to the bowl with the butter. Mix well, beating with a whisk or a hand mixer, until you have a smooth, creamy, and fluffy dough. Incorporate the diced pineapple, raisins, shredded coconut, and pecans into the dough using a spatula.

3. To assemble the tamales, place a corn husk on your work surface with the wide end facing toward you. Place about ¼ cup (60 g) of the dough in the center of the corn husk, closer to the bottom of the husk (the wide end). Using the back of a large spoon, evenly spread the dough toward the left, right, and bottom edges. The dough should reach all the way to the bottom edge (or just before it) but leave an inch (2.5 cm) of space on the left and right sides. Fold the right and left sides of the corn husk in toward the center, overlapping each other and completely covering the dough and the filling. Next, fold the narrow end of the husk up toward the center. Repeat this process with the remaining 11 corn husks and dough. I usually line up the formed tamales on a tray as I make them.

4. To steam the tamales, place a steamer rack inside a large stockpot. Add enough warm water so that it almost reaches the steamer rack, then line the rack with a layer of corn husks. Place the tamales

in the pot in an upright position, with the open ends facing up. Cover them with a generous layer of husks, then cover the pot. Steam the tamales for about 45 minutes over medium heat. During the steaming, check the pot to see if it has enough water (be careful when removing the lid), adding more if needed (see Notas). To check if the tamales are ready, remove one from the pot, wait 5 minutes, then open it. If the husk separates easily from the dough when you open it, that means that the tamal is ready. If the dough sticks to the husk, place it back in the pot and cook for 15 more minutes.

5. Serve the tamales while still hot; just let them rest for 5 minutes so the dough can firm up.

NOTAS

* *If you want to make larger tamales, you will need to steam them for about an hour.*

* *If you need to add more water to the pot when steaming the tamales, make sure to pour it as close to the wall of the pot as possible, avoiding the tamales. If water gets into the tamales, they will lose their flavor and the dough will be soggy.*

* *You can store the tamales in plastic bags in your freezer for up to 4 months. To reheat them, allow them to defrost, then place them in a steamer for 10 to 15 minutes. You can also pop them in the microwave on a high setting for about 1 minute.*

AGUA DE HORCHATA

Horchata

A sweet and refreshing drink, horchata is often served during lunch or dinner, or enjoyed by itself throughout the day, especially during the hot summer season. Its fresh, creamy flavor makes it an excellent beverage to have on hand when you find yourself eating a dish that is spicy. Horchata is the most prevalent of the aguas frescas in Mexico. It is usually made with rice, cinnamon, and vanilla extract, but in the south of the country, you can also find it made with almond or coconut. Some people like to add milk in the preparation of this drink, like me, while others prefer it without.

PREP TIME: 5 minutes plus 8 hours resting time	**YIELD:** 3 quarts (2.8 L)

2 cups (360 g) long-grain white rice

1 Mexican cinnamon stick

4 cups (1 quart/950 ml) hot water

1 cup (240 ml) whole milk (optional)

2 teaspoons vanilla extract

6 cups (1½ quarts/1.4 L) water

¼ cup (150 g) sugar

Ice cubes, to serve

Ground cinnamon, for dusting (optional)

1. Place the rice and cinnamon stick in a large glass bowl and add the hot water. Cover the bowl with a dish or plastic wrap, then let it soak for 8 hours, or overnight.

2. Pour the rice, cinnamon, and water into a blender, and blend until it becomes a smooth, watery paste.

3. Using a strainer, strain the mixture into a wide-mouth pitcher, stirring to help the liquid pass through.

4. Add the milk (if using), vanilla extract, and the 6 cups (1½ quarts/1.4 L) water. Stir in the sugar, then refrigerate until serving.

5. Stir before serving because the rice mix tends to settle at the bottom. Serve in glasses with ice cubes and dust with the cinnamon (if using).

NOTAS

* *If you have a high-performance blender, you won't need to rest the rice to soften it, as the blender will be powerful enough to grind the hard rice grains. Additionally, you probably won't need to use a strainer to strain the rice water, as the rice mixture will be finely processed.*

* *Always taste the drink before adding the sugar in step 4. You might prefer more or less sugar than the amount indicated in the ingredients.*

* *If you find that the consistency of the horchata is too thick or dense for your taste, simply add more water.*

* *This drink can be refrigerated for up to 2 days.*

AGUA DE JAMAICA

Hibiscus Iced Tea

Jamaica (hibiscus) flowers are used in different parts of the world to make a cold or hot tea sweetened with sugar. In Mexico, besides being one of the most popular of the aguas frescas, many people drink it for its health benefits, believing that it can lower high blood pressure. It also has diuretic effects. The flavor of this drink is on the tart side, similar to the flavor of cranberry juice. Of the many aguas frescas, this one is my favorite. I also like that it's easy to prepare, and you can keep it in the refrigerator for several days.

PREP TIME: 25 minutes plus 2 hours chilling time	**COOK TIME:** 5 minutes	**YIELD:** 2 quarts (1.9 L)

1¼ cups (50 g) dried hibiscus flowers

7 cups (1.7 L) water, divided

½ cup (100 g) sugar

2 cups (280 g) ice cubes

1. Place the dried hibiscus flowers in a small saucepan with 3 cups (710 ml) of the water. Bring to a boil over medium-high heat, then reduce the heat to medium-low and gently simmer for about 5 minutes. Remove the pan from the heat and let the hibiscus tea rest for at least 25 minutes.

2. Strain the liquid into a pitcher and add the remaining 4 cups (1 quart/950 ml) water and the sugar. You can adjust the amount of added water if you feel that the drink is too tart for your taste.

3. Stir the ingredients, add the ice cubes, and then let it chill for at least 2 hours.

NOTAS

✱ If you're in a hurry, you can speed up the process of resting the hot tea by adding 4 to 5 cups (885 g to 1.1 kg) ice cubes instead of the 4 cups (1 quart/950 ml) water in step 2.

✱ Always taste the drink before adding the sugar in step 2. You might prefer more or less sugar than the amount indicated in the ingredients.

✱ This drink can be refrigerated for up to 4 days.

AGUA DE TAMARINDO

Tamarind Drink

In Mexico, tamarind is used to prepare cold drinks, hot drinks, and many sweet treats, like ice cream and paletas. Tamarind can also be used as a sauce for some dishes, but the most common use for it is to make this refreshing drink. In the United States, you can buy tamarind pods at Asian, Indian, Caribbean, and African markets, since it is widely known in those cultures; you can also buy them online.

PREP TIME: 10 minutes plus 2 hours resting time	**COOK TIME:** 15 minutes	**YIELD:** 2 quarts (1.9 L)

8 ounces (225 g) tamarind pods (about 2 cups)

8 cups (2 quarts/1.9 L) water, divided

½ cup (100 g) sugar

Ice cubes, to serve

1. Peel the tamarind pods, making sure to remove most of the shells.

2. Add the peeled tamarind pods and 4 cups (1 quart/950 ml) of the water to a medium saucepan over medium-high heat. Bring to a boil, then reduce the heat and simmer for about 15 minutes. Remove from the heat and set aside. Let the tamarind steep for about 2 hours; this will help soften the pulp and cool down the water.

3. Use a strainer to strain the pulp into a wide-mouth pitcher. You will need to use your fingers in order to get as much of the pulp as possible through the strainer. You should be left with only the seeds and veins in the strainer; the rest of the pulp will be in the pitcher.

4. Add the sugar and remaining 4 cups (1 quart/950 ml) water, stir, and then refrigerate until serving.

5. Stir before serving. Serve in glasses with ice cubes.

NOTAS

✳ *If you can't find tamarind pods, some ethnic markets sell tamarind pulp that is pressed down into a brick and wrapped in plastic. To make the drink using this product, soften the pulp with warm water and then proceed to step 2.*

✳ *Always taste the drink before adding the sugar in step 4. You might prefer more or less sugar than the amount indicated in the ingredients.*

✳ *This drink can be refrigerated for up to 4 days.*

ATOLE BLANCO

White Atole

Atoles are hot drinks that are usually thickened with fresh masa harina or corn starch. I've found that people in urban areas prefer both versions, but in rural areas, corn-flour atoles are most common. This drink is a portion of the daily diet for many people living in rural areas of Mexico, where it is consumed for breakfast or dinner. Since pre-Hispanic times, the atole has often been considered more of a meal than a drink. To this day, some farm workers will only drink an atole for breakfast before going out to work in the field. This thick and hearty drink is sure to make you feel better, especially during the winter months.

PREP TIME: 5 minutes	**COOK TIME:** 15 minutes	**YIELD:** 1 quart (950 ml)

4 cups (1 quart/950 ml) whole milk

⅓ cup (65 g) sugar

6 tablespoons (45 g) masa harina

¾ cup (180 ml) water

1. Mix together the milk and sugar in a large saucepan. Turn the heat to medium-high.

2. In a small bowl, mix the masa harina with the water. Stir well to dissolve any lumps.

3. Once the milk comes to a boil, slowly whisk in the mixture of corn flour and water. Bring to a boil once again, then reduce the heat to medium-low and keep simmering until the atole has thickened, 6 to 8 minutes, stirring occasionally to keep it from sticking to the bottom of the saucepan. Once the atole starts to cool, it will thicken even more.

4. Serve in mugs. Be careful before drinking, as its thick consistency keeps the drink very hot.

NOTAS

✳ *I prefer whole milk, but you can use any other type of milk that you prefer.*

✳ *When I was growing up, my mom used to give us this drink (without the milk) when we were ill. To make a simple atole, substitute the amount of milk with water.*

✳ *The brand or type of masa harina you use will affect the thickness of the final drink.*

ATOLE DE ARROZ

Rice Atole

Atoles are not only made using corn flour as a thickening agent, as with this recipe for this warm rice drink. *Atole de arroz* is a common remedy for stomach ailments when made with only water, cinnamon, and a little sugar. It is also given to people who are following a bland diet, or for those suffering from intestinal flu. Of course, you can also make it just to enjoy it.

PREP TIME: 5 minutes	**COOK TIME:** 30 minutes	**YIELD:** 1½ quarts (1.4 L)

½ cup (95 g) short-grain white rice

3 cups (710 ml) water

1 Mexican cinnamon stick

3 cups (710 ml) whole milk

Scant ½ cup (85 g) sugar

Ground cinnamon, for dusting (optional)

NOTA *If you have leftover atole, wait for it to completely cool and then store it in the refrigerator for up to 3 days. Reheat it in a medium saucepan over low heat for 10 minutes, or until warm.*

1. Place the rice, water, and cinnamon stick in a medium saucepan. Turn the heat to medium-high and bring to a boil. Reduce the heat to low and cook for 20 minutes, stirring occasionally.

2. Add the milk and sugar, stir to combine, then remove half the rice.

3. Place the rice you removed from the saucepan into a blender and blend until smooth.

4. Return this rice mixture to the pan and continue cooking over medium-high heat until it comes to a boil again and has slightly thickened.

5. Remove the cinnamon stick and serve in mugs. Dust with a little ground cinnamon (if using).

CHAMPURRADO

This recipe is for the classic water–based *champurrado*, but you can also make it using milk. You can even add cloves or orange peel for extra flavor. Whichever way you choose to prepare this popular drink, I'm sure you'll enjoy sharing it with your loved ones.

PREP TIME: 5 minutes	**COOK TIME:** 30 minutes	**YIELD:** 8 servings

8 cups (2 quarts/1.9 L) water, divided

5 ounces (140 g) piloncillo or ½ cup (100 g) dark brown sugar

1 Mexican cinnamon stick

2 Mexican chocolate tablets (about 6.3 ounces/175 g)

¾ cup (95 g) masa harina

NOTAS

* *You can also use milk instead of water, or half water and half milk.*

* *For an even thicker consistency, use the amounts in the recipe and then add 2 to 4 more tablespoons (10 to 20 g) of masa harina mixed with ½ cup (120 ml) water (make sure the corn flour is completely dissolved).*

1. Place 6 cups (1½ quarts/1.4 L) of the water in a large saucepan over medium-high heat with the piloncillo and cinnamon stick. Bring to a boil, then reduce the heat to medium and let simmer for about 10 minutes, until the piloncillo has melted. If you're using dark brown sugar, this step will take less time because the sugar will dissolve in about 4 to 5 minutes.

2. Add the chocolate tablets and continue simmering for 5 minutes, stirring occasionally, until they dissolve.

3. Meanwhile, pour the remaining 2 cups (480 ml) water into a medium bowl and add the masa harina. Mix well with an egg beater (if possible) to avoid forming any lumps. It should have a creamy texture.

4. When the chocolate has completely dissolved, slowly pour the masa harina mixture into the saucepan while stirring, to make sure there are no lumps. If you want to be safe, use a strainer to pour in the mixture.

5. Increase the heat to medium-high until the champurrado starts boiling, then reduce the heat to low and gently simmer, stirring constantly. After 6 to 8 minutes, the mixture will begin to thicken. Allow it to cook for 5 more minutes, then remove from the heat.

6. Serve in mugs. Be careful before drinking, as its thick consistency keeps the drink very hot.

CAFÉ DE OLLA

Mexican Spiced Coffee

Café de olla is a Mexican spiced coffee made with ground coffee, cinnamon, and a raw dark sugar called *piloncillo*. Traditionally, this coffee is made using a large clay pot, called *olla de barro*, over a firewood stove. At her farm, my grandma used a large, blue enamel pot. It always sat there next to the firewood stove, ready to welcome any visitor, no matter the season or time of day. This recipe brings back sweet memories of my grandma and her farm in Veracruz.

PREP TIME: 8 minutes	**COOK TIME:** 7 minutes	**YIELD:** 1 quart (950 ml)

4 cups (1 quart/950 ml) water

½ Mexican cinnamon stick

3 ounces (85 g) piloncillo or ⅓ cup (70 g) dark brown sugar

¼ cup (20 g) ground coffee (dark Mexican coffee is best)

1. Place the water, cinnamon, and piloncillo in a medium saucepan over medium heat. Simmer until the piloncillo has dissolved, about 7 minutes (about 5 minutes if using dark brown sugar).
2. Increase the heat to medium-high. When the water starts boiling, add the coffee and immediately turn off the heat and stir. Cover the pot and let the coffee steep for 5 minutes.
3. To serve, pour the coffee through a strainer into mugs.

NOTAS

- *This is the most common version of café de olla. You can sometimes find it with the addition of cloves, orange peel, or anise seeds.*
- *When buying piloncillo, make sure to look for the pure version, which has a dark color. Some stores carry a look-alike version that is just plain sugar in a cone shape, lacking the flavor and nutrients of the real piloncillo.*
- *To easily cut the piloncillo, warm it first to soften it.*
- *If you would like to add some spirits, a coffee liqueur like Kahlúa is a good choice.*

CHOCOLATE CALIENTE

Mexican Hot Chocolate

Chocolate has had a very special place in Mexican culture since the time of the Aztecs. Hot chocolate is often a companion to special meals and treats during celebrations, such as with savory tamales on Día de Muertos and Buñuelos (page 152) during Christmastime. However, you do not need to wait for a special occasion to enjoy a delicious, frothy cup of hot chocolate.

PREP TIME: 2 minutes	**COOK TIME:** 8 minutes	**YIELD:** 4 servings

4 cups (1 quart/950 ml) whole milk

1½ Mexican chocolate tablets (about 4¾ ounces/130 g)

¼ teaspoon ground cinnamon

1 teaspoon vanilla extract

1. Place the milk, chocolate tablets, and ground cinnamon in a medium saucepan over low heat. Simmer for about 6 minutes, stirring occasionally, until the chocolate dissolves.

2. Froth the mixture using a molinillo or a whisk to form a nice foam.

3. Just before serving, stir in the vanilla extract and then pour into mugs.

NOTA *If you prefer your chocolate on the sweeter side, add some sugar to the saucepan after the chocolate dissolves in step 1, but make sure to taste the hot chocolate first.*

PONCHE NAVIDEÑO
Mexican Christmas Punch

Ponche Navideño is a traditional hot drink made in Mexico during the holidays. It is prepared with water and a variety of fresh and dried fruits. Other ingredients include sugar cane sticks, cinnamon, piloncillo, and sometimes hibiscus. While a few people might add aromatics, like anise seeds and chamomile flowers, many adults prefer to add a splash of spirits, such as rum, brandy, or aguardiente. I love the aroma of the simmering fruits and spices coming out of the kitchen when I make this drink. Delicious and warming, this fruit punch is the perfect way to bring the flavors of Christmas into your home.

PREP TIME: 10 minutes	**COOK TIME:** 1 hour 10 minutes	**YIELD:** 12 servings

1 gallon (3.8 litres) water

1 large piloncillo cone or 12 ounces (340 g) dark brown sugar

3 Mexican cinnamon sticks

1 pound (450 g) tejocote

1½ pounds (675 g) guavas (about 12 guavas)

1 medium apple, peeled, cored, and chopped

¾ cup (100 g) chopped pitted prunes

3 sugar cane sticks (about 4½ inches/11.5 cm long each), split into quarters

1 cup peeled tamarind pods (120 g) or dried hibiscus flowers (40 g)

1 cup (225 g) cored and chopped pears

½ cup (70 g) raisins

Rum, to taste (optional)

1. Add the water, piloncillo, and cinnamon sticks to a large stockpot over medium-high heat. If you're using fresh tejocotes, add them in this step, as they take longer to cook and soften. Bring to a boil, then reduce the heat to low and cook for about 10 minutes.

2. Stir in the guavas, apple, and prunes, along with the sugar cane sticks and tamarind pods. If you're using canned tejocotes, add them now. Finally, add the pears and raisins (these take the shortest time to cook). Simmer for about 1 hour.

3. Serve the hot punch in mugs, ladling in some of the fruit as well. Serve each mug with one of the sugar cane sticks. Add the rum (if using).

NOTAS

* If you cannot find all the ingredients, like the tejocotes or sugar cane sticks, you can make this drink without them.

* For this punch, I use tamarind pods most often, but sometimes I substitute hibiscus flowers; I rarely use both of them at the same time.

* If you live in an area where some of the ingredients are difficult to find, some Latin stores occasionally sell canned punch ingredients in a syrup. Additionally, sugar cane sticks can be found at many Asian supermarkets.

INDEX

ACKNOWLEDGMENTS

Many of the recipes in this book wouldn't have been possible without all the cooks who shared their knowledge with me along this long road called life, and I'd like to give my thanks to all of them. To the *taquero* at the street corner of my neighborhood, when I was living in Monterrey, who told me how to make beef tacos; to the woman that used to sell *tacos de guisados* next to the highway and gave me tips for cooking *asado de puerco*; and to Doña Hortencia, who used to make dozens of flour tortillas for her family and taught me how to make them. To the special women in my family: my mom, Ernestina, my dear grandma, Sixta, and all my aunts, especially my Tía Nono, who taught me the joy of cooking.

A special thanks to Erin Canning for your patience and for believing I could actually write a cookbook, and to everyone involved at The Quarto Group.

To Mariana and Manuel Arciniega, for the beautiful gift of designing the logo for Mexico in My Kitchen, you are both very talented. To my exceptional friend Leticia Alaníz, for taking the portrait pictures that capture my everyday spirit.

A huge thanks to the loyal readers of Mexico in My Kitchen, who have been requesting this book for some years now. Thank you for your constant support and for keeping me inspired and motivated to keep sharing our Mexican gastronomy with the world. This book is for you and your families.

To my husband, for seeing the potential I had and for helping me since the beginning of my blog, as my English was and still is a work in progress.

And finally, to my son David A., who was my eyes behind the camera, my text editor, and sometimes even the dishwasher while we created this book. Thank you, *mijo*, I couldn't have done it without you. You know that this book is also yours.

Thank you, all, and keep passing these recipes to the next generations.

ABOUT THE AUTHOR

MELY MARTÍNEZ was born in the coastal city of Tampico, Tamaulipas, Mexico, and was raised in a family of eight children. She began to help out in her mom's kitchen at a young age, and spent the long, tropical summers at her grandmother's ranch in the state of Veracruz.

During her time as a rural schoolteacher in the south of Mexico, Mely's exposure to different regional customs allowed her culinary interest to grow even deeper. Throughout her life, she has lived in and traveled to many of Mexico's states and regions, always visiting the local markets and street stands, where she believes you can find the heart of every city's cuisine.

In 2008, she started her website, Mexico in My Kitchen, where she shares Mexican recipes so that they can be passed down and preserved for new generations, as well as shared with all food lovers. Besides writing for her website, Mely enjoys traveling and gardening, as well as attending seminars, festivals, and other events related to Mexican culture and gastronomy. She also serves as a consultant to chefs and restauranteurs around the world.

She lives in Dallas, Texas.